The Night
the Revolution Began

The Boston Tea Party, 1773

by Wesley S. Griswold

Rally Mohawks! bring out your axes,
And tell King George we'll pay no taxes
*   On his foreign tea;*
His threats are vain, and vain to think
To force our girls and wives to drink
*   His vile Bohea!*
         —Fragment of a Boston tavern song (1773–74)
         inspired by the Boston Tea Party

THE STEPHEN GREENE PRESS
BRATTLEBORO, VERMONT

This book has been produced in the United States of America: designed by R. L. Dothard Associates, composed by Heffernan Press, printed and bound by Halliday Lithograph Corporation. It is published by the Stephen Greene Press, Brattleboro, Vermont 05301.

Library of Congress Catalog Card Number: 72-81524
International Standard Book Number: 0-8289-0168-6

For Marjorie & Arthur Griswold

Acknowledgments

Once again, in concluding the writing of a book, I feel impelled to express my gratitude and delight at the rich resources of the University Research Library of the University of California, Los Angeles, and my thankful appreciation of the privilege of utilizing them. The very few needed items that it did not have readily available were cheerfully and promptly lent me by the University's library at Berkeley. It is sad indeed to contemplate the present dangerous threat to the continuing excellence of the University's library collection from ill-informed budget trimmers.

I also wish to thank the National Gallery of Art, Washington, D.C.; the Museum of Fine Arts, Boston; the Trustees of Dartmouth College; the Massachusetts Historical Society; the Trustees of Harvard University; and the Wichita Art Museum for their gracious permission to reproduce in this book various historical portraits from their collections.

Contents

List of Illustrations

Foreword

IT CAN BE said with confidence—though, from my standpoint, with rather wistful regret—that no one knows now (or perhaps ever did) precisely who was present at the Boston Tea Party or everything that happened there. It was a strenuous but surprisingly quiet affair. A thin young moon, which provided little illumination, set before the Party was over. The daring business of destroying the East India Company's property within a few yards of the commander-in-chief of His Majesty's naval squadrons in American waters, and practically under the guns of three of his men-of-war, took place largely by lantern and torchlight.

No eyewitness account preserved more than the meagerest details for posterity, and then only from the viewpoint of an idle spectator on the wharf who couldn't have seen very well what was going on. No participant, more's the pity, confided his derring-do to a diary— or if he did, it was soon lost or destroyed, for no manuscript of that nature has ever turned up in the ensuing two hundred years. Peter Edes, son of Benjamin Edes, printer of the Boston *Gazette* at the time of the Tea Party and unquestionably a participant in it, once stated that his father had for some time afterward kept locked in his desk a complete list of those who took part. Maybe so, but the list has never been found.

The reader will find an alphabetical roster of purported Tea Party participants given in the Appendix. Their names, though, were culled long ago from the uncertain memories of a trio of gaffers, one of whom was nearly one hundred and fourteen years old at the time his recollections were set down (1850), and from the conceivably embroidered traditions of several venerable Boston families. However, even the family tales were not collected and printed until more than a hundred years after the event.

Provided that one had been a party to the Party, there was ample reason to keep mum about it until after the Revolution. As long as the outcome of that struggle remained in doubt, one was potentially subject, at best, to civil suit by the East India Company for the recovery of damages. At worst, one could be held guilty of treason, the penalty for which was hanging. It is curious, though, that boasting didn't begin as soon as the fighting was over and America had won its independence. Why keep quiet then if one had had a hand in starting the Revolution? Perhaps the threat of civil suit still persisted, but the continuing silence of most of the surviving participants during their lifetimes remains a mystery. It hardly seems human.

As late as 1819, John Adams declared that he had never known the name of a single man who helped dump the hated tea overboard that night. With all proper respect for President Adams, I find that statement questionable. He was too close to the principal plotters not to have learned the identity of at least a few of them. Perhaps by 1819 he could no longer remember. In any event, he didn't furnish any enlightenment on the subject to future Americans.

The account of the Boston Tea Party that comprises the third section of this book is therefore largely an interwoven fabric of old men's recollections, recorded respectively in 1835 and 1850, and of anecdotes passed down in certain families from one generation to the next and finally published in 1884. It is bolstered by a few contemporary letters and laconic newspaper accounts and by certain undeniable facts, such as the phase of the moon and the status of the tide. It is also the most complete account known to date. But it cannot be claimed to be the whole truth, merely what seems likely to have been quite close to it.

The opportunity for anyone to write a complete, accurate description of what happened in immediate preparation for the famous Tea Party and, subsequently, aboard the *Dartmouth*, *Beaver*, and *Eleanor* on that distant December evening of 1773 has long been lost forever.

W.S.G.

Principals

ANTI-ADMINISTRATION

John Adams, lawyer, cousin of Samuel Adams

Samuel Adams, politician, mastermind of American independence movement

John Andrews, merchant and diarist

John Avery, Jr., secretary of militant, secret "Loyal Nine," who signed dictatorial handbills "O.C."

Colonel Isaac Barré, Irish M.P., steadfast friend of Americans

James Bowdoin, merchant, prominent member of Governor's Council of Massachusetts

Captain Hezekiah Coffin, master of the tea-carrying brig *Beaver*

William Cooper, Boston Town Clerk

Thomas Cushing, Speaker of Massachusetts House of Representatives

William Dennie, merchant and ship owner

William Dowdeswell, British M.P., persistent defender of Americans

Benjamin Edes, printer of Boston *Gazette*

Benjamin Franklin, Boston-born London agent for Massachusetts and other colonies

John Hancock, merchant and ship owner

Alexander Hodgdon, mate of tea ship *Dartmouth*

Arthur Lee, Virginian agent for Massachusetts in London, colleague of Franklin's

Ebenezer Mackintosh, shoemaker, leader of Boston mob under Loyal Nine's direction

William Molineux, Irish-born Boston merchant and brawler

James Otis, distinguished lawyer of fading intellect

Josiah Quincy, Jr., lawyer, orator, fatally ill of tuberculosis

Paul Revere, silversmith, engraver, courier for Boston Committee of Correspondence

John Rowe, merchant, diarist, owner of tea ship *Eleanor*

Samuel Phillips Savage, moderator of crucial Boston mass meetings of December 14–16, 1773

John Scollay, merchant, chairman of Boston Board of Selectmen

Captain James Scott, master of John Hancock's ship *Hayley*

James Warren, Plymouth politician, husband of Mercy Warren, close friend of John and Samuel Adams

Dr. Joseph Warren, popular Boston physician and orator

Mercy Warren, poetical dramatist, intimate friend of Abigail and John Adams, eventual historian of the Revolution

Jonathan Williams, moderator of Boston mass meetings of November 29–30, 1773

Dr. Hugh Williamson, Philadelphia physician and worker for American independence, eyewitness of the Boston Tea Party

Dr. Thomas Young, John Adams's family physician and close friend

AN APOLITICAL GO-BETWEEN

John Singleton Copley, eminent artist, who loathed politics and controversy but as a son-in-law of Richard Clarke, eldest tea consignee, was moved to volunteer to serve as emissary between the Boston mass meetings of November 29–30, 1773, and the tea consignees

PRO-ADMINISTRATION

Captain James Bruce, master of tea ship *Eleanor*

Dr. Benjamin Church, ostensible Boston revolutionary, paid informer for General Gage

Isaac Winslow Clarke, tea consignee, younger son of Richard Clarke

Jonathan Clarke, tea consignee, elder son of Richard Clarke

Richard Clarke, senior tea consignee, owner of brig *William*, brother-in-law of Chief Justice Peter Oliver

Lord Dartmouth, William Legge, British Secretary of State for the American Department, stepbrother of Lord North

Abraham Dupuis, London banker, financial underwriter for the Clarkes

Benjamin Faneuil, Jr., tea consignee

General Thomas Gage, commander-in-chief of British troops in North America, acting Governor of Massachusetts beginning in May, 1774

George III, decent, mediocre and stubborn King of Great Britain, Ireland, etc.

Captain James Hall, master of tea ship *Dartmouth*

Ann Hulton, assiduous letter-writer, sister of a British customs official at Boston

Elisha Hutchinson, tea consignee, brother and partner of Thomas Hutchinson, Jr.

Thomas Hutchinson, Royal Governor of the Province of Massachusetts Bay, a native son more British than the British

Thomas Hutchinson, Jr., tea consignee, eldest son of the Governor

Lieutenant-Colonel Alexander Leslie, commander of the 64th Regiment of Foot, stationed at Castle William in Boston Harbor

Captain Joseph Royal Loring, master of the Clarkes' brig *William*

Admiral John Montagu, commander-in-chief of British naval forces in North America

Lord Frederick North, Prime Minister of Great Britain, pawn of George III, stepbrother of Lord Dartmouth

Andrew Oliver, Lieutenant-Governor of Massachusetts, brother-in-law of Governor Hutchinson

Peter Oliver, Chief Justice of Massachusetts, brother-in-law of Richard Clarke

William Palmer, London merchant-banker, financial underwriter for the Hutchinson brothers

Francis Rotch, Quaker owner of tea ship *Dartmouth*

William Tryon, Royal Governor of New York and frequent confidant of Governor Thomas Hutchinson

Brook Watson, London merchant-banker, financial underwriter for Benjamin Faneuil, Jr., and Joshua Winslow.

The Antagonists
(1763–November 2, 1773)

I

HEAVY pounding on the front door of Richard Clarke's stone mansion sounded shockingly loud as it echoed through School Street, sleeping under a high moon. The hour was one o'clock on a frosty Tuesday morning, November 2, 1773, in the town of Boston.

Clarke, a prominent tea merchant past middle age, awoke confusedly. After fumbling into a dressing gown, he moved with caution across the darkened bedroom to a window. From there he could look down upon the steps that curved upward to the broad, columned portico of his residence, closest eastern neighbor of King's Chapel.

The imperious knocking had now ceased. In the white light of the moon, only three nights past its full phase, Clarke saw two men standing near the top of the steps, their faces raised expectantly. He pushed open the window, admitting a gush of chill, salty air, and called out haughtily, "What do you want?"

"We have an important letter for you—from the country," one of the men shouted.

Clarke hesitated, puzzled that a letter should require delivery at this unsuitable hour. Then he pulled the window shut and roused a servant to fetch the letter for him. It might be an urgent message from his kinsman and close friend Thomas Hutchinson, Royal Governor of the Province of Massachusetts Bay, then in prudent retreat from resentful Bostonians at his country house in Milton, a few miles to the southeast. Instead, when Clarke unfolded and read the letter by candlelight, he found it to be an infuriating communiqué, from a source he regarded as scurrilous and contemptible. This was the message:

1

Boston, 1st Nov., 1773

RICHARD CLARKE & SON:

The Freemen of this Province understand, from good authority, that there is a quantity of tea consigned to your house by the East India Company, which is destructive to the happiness of every well-wisher to his country. It is therefore expected that you personally appear at Liberty Tree, on Wednesday next, at twelve o'clock at noon day, to make a public resignation of your commission, agreeable to a notification of this day for that purpose.

Fail not, upon your peril.

O.C., *Sec'y.*

"Wednesday next," by this late hour, had become tomorrow. The Liberty Tree was a giant oak, its branches stretching over a fair portion of Hanover Square.

[Planted in 1646, three years before King Charles I lost his head, it had grown to be the most noticeable tree in Boston. Since 1765, the Sons of Liberty—a loose confederation of certain local political and social clubs; a band of obstreperous malcontents, as Clarke and his friends viewed them—had made a point of holding their rallies beneath it, occasionally trimming its immense lower branches with effigies of public figures whom they particularly disliked.]

The initials "O.C." at the close of the message were meaningless to Clarke. (What they stood for is still a mystery, though it is certain that they were not intended to be the initials of any individual known to the author of the message.) The arrogant style and self-righteous tone of the text were disagreeably familiar to the tea merchant, however. They were typical of manifestoes from the Sons of Liberty, who had grown in boldness until they behaved as if they were the true government of Massachusetts—as, indeed, they very nearly were.

Clarke had become accustomed to reading their inflammatory open letters in Boston newspapers and seeing their subversive broadsides pasted to trees and the corners of buildings. They seemed determined, these exasperating Sons of Liberty, to stir up trouble with King George III's officials in Boston, inciting street mobs, alienating Parliament, and offending the King himself. As a contented and loyal citizen of the British Empire, Clarke resented them with deep indignation and scorn.

[Also, he could scarcely have failed to recall, as he contemplated the officious summons in hand, that it was under the Liberty Tree in 1765, at the height of Boston's revolt against the Stamp Act, that the Sons had forced his friend Andrew Oliver, now Lieutenant-Governor, to undergo public humiliation. They had marched Oliver bareheaded through the streets in an icy rain to stand before a crowd of two thousand hostile fellow-townsmen at the Liberty Tree and abjectly resign his appointment as stamp master. Was something similar now in store for Richard Clarke?]

As Clarke stood in his nightshirt and dressing gown, sputtering in anger over the impudent, anonymous summons he held, he was not yet aware that nearly identical messages had been delivered at about the same hour to four other men of the town—the accidental associates of himself and his sons in a brash and foolish, unplanned commercial venture soon to end in a debacle significant to the course of American history. Nor could Clarke know that already a fresh crop of broadsides, the latest edict from the Sons of Liberty, was fluttering in the wind on Boston trees and street corners.

To the Freemen of this and the other Towns in the Province.

GENTLEMEN:

You are desired to meet at Liberty Tree next Wednesday at twelve o'clock at noon day, then and there to hear the persons to whom the tea shipped by the East India Company is consigned make a public resignation of their office as consignees, upon oath. And also swear that they will reship any teas that may be consigned to them by the said Company by the first vessel sailing for London.

Boston, Novr. 1st, 1773   O.C., *Sec'y.*

At the bottom of the broadside appeared a stylized drawing of a hand, its index finger pointing to the warning "Show me the man that dares take this down."

Whoever had written Clarke's nocturnal message had addressed it to "Richard Clarke & Son," ostensibly overlooking the fact that there were two sons in the firm. More likely the writer was aware that only one of the sons, Isaac, aged twenty-seven, was in Boston at the time. Richard's elder son, Jonathan, thirty, the partner on whom

he most heavily relied, had sailed for England in the spring to attend
the East India Company's seasonal tea auctions in London to buy for
his firm.

So, at the moment in question on the morning of November 2nd,
Jonathan Clarke was far beyond the reach of messages from the Sons
of Liberty. He was, in fact, six weeks out of London, homeward bound
through stormy gray seas aboard John Hancock's new little ship
Hayley—and lucky for him, as the Sons of Liberty suspected, quite
wrongly, that Jonathan Clarke had been a plotter in the scheme that
they were now denouncing as "destructive to the happiness of every
well-wisher to his country," and planned to give him an exceedingly
unpleasant reception when he returned home.

[Before that Wednesday afternoon was very far advanced, the first
confrontation between the Sons of Liberty and the tea consignees
would occur, but it would not take place under the Liberty Tree.
It would end in a rough-and-tumble fight in the Clarke warehouse on
King Street, the broad thoroughfare that led straight up into the heart
of Boston from Long Wharf, the town's chief anchorage.]

II

The scheme that seemed so destructive to Boston's high-handed Sons
of Liberty was one that appeared to hold a double menace for Americans. It was a wily new attempt, the fourth in ten years, to force them
to pay a British tax that many of them believed to be unconstitutional.
In addition, for the first time, it posed an immediate threat to the
livelihood of some of their businessmen, and a potential threat to
that of nearly all of them.

In briefest terms, the plan involved a previously untried method
of marketing tea in America and collecting a longstanding, but often
evaded, tax of three pence per pound on it. (Ironically, the scheme had
not been hatched, or even envisioned, by any member of the small
group of Boston merchants whom the Sons of Liberty were now
threatening.)

For nearly one hundred and fifty years after the first American
colonies were established, Parliament had not taxed them for income,

following a policy that one British statesman appropriately called "salutary neglect." There had been customs duties, to keep other nations out of the rich British-American trade, but no taxes imposed primarily for revenue. In the decade following 1763, however, the British government made four sporadic efforts to collect taxes from the Americans for general income purposes.

The official justification given for these moves was that the money was needed to maintain a standing army of ten thousand British troops for the defense of the colonies. It seemed only fair to Parliament, burdened with what then seemed a huge war debt and faced with irate and balky British taxpayers, that the Americans should pay for their own protection. The Americans, on the other hand, saw no further need for British troops on their shores, now that the French and Indian forces had been thoroughly defeated. Furthermore, their political leaders believed, and repeatedly stated in reasonably respectful petitions to the King, that Parliament had no constitutional right to tax them; that only taxes devised by themselves for themselves were legitimate.

In a century and a half of "salutary neglect," Americans had become among the most independent political beings on earth. They had far more true liberty than their British counterparts. They were generally satisfied to be citizens of the British Empire, but their provincial charters assured them that they were entitled to all the rights and privileges of Englishmen, and they were increasingly sensitive to any implications that they were second-class citizens. One of the foremost of their rights, as they saw it, was that of being taxed by their own representatives.

Since it was admittedly impractical to send American representatives to Parliament, even if they should be welcomed there—the communications gap would have rendered them largely unresponsive to their constituents' changing needs and opinions—the Americans believed that they should be taxed solely by their provincial legislatures. Needless to say, taxation from that source would be most unlikely to furnish lavish funds for the disposal of Parliament, which most Americans believed, and with reason, to be largely corrupt and unresponsive to the public will.

In consequence, every attempt by Parliament to tax the colonists had failed. The tax laws either had been evaded by smuggling, as was the time-honored practice in Britain; flouted by riotous assaults on the persons of would-be tax collectors or on the properties of other royal appointees; or negated by mass refusals to buy all goods imported from Britain, whether they bore a tax or not.

[During this last means of resistance, which lasted from 1768 to 1770, Harvard and Princeton students had worn homespun rather than broadcloth, Yale students had forsworn drinking foreign wines, and patriotic ladies had taken to brewing "tea" from raspberry leaves, or even less palatable substitutes for their beloved black Bohea from China.

Further, even the most responsible citizens didn't hesitate to break the law imposing a tax on tea. Young John Adams, with a touch of the whimsical humor that occasionally lightened his earnest nature, is said to have remarked to a hostess during this period, "Is it lawful for a weary traveler to refresh himself with a dish of tea, provided it has been honestly smuggled or paid no duties?" The lady said no, rather severely, declaring with pride that everybody in her household had given up tea; she would be glad, however, to serve him coffee.]

American merchants patriotically, but restively, suffered a painful dearth of business during this spell of non-importation. More significantly, British merchants angrily complained to Parliament about their own loss of trade with the colonies.

Parliament had finally felt obliged, in every instance, to rescind the offending law—with one important exception: the tax on tea was deliberately kept in force, as a token of Parliament's right to impose it. Parliament's right to be the Empire's supreme legislature was never doubted by any British lawmaker, no matter how benignly he might view the Americans. Members of Parliament believed in the eighteenth-century mercantilist philosophy that colonies existed for the benefit of the mother country. The crucial question argued was whether or not it was expedient to try to tax the "touchy" colonials. That valiant Dubliner, Colonel Isaac Barré, who had fondly referred to Americans as "sons of liberty" when he was arguing in their behalf against the Stamp Act in 1765, once illuminated the heart of the matter with a pithy phrase: "Keep your hands out of the pockets of the Americans, and they will be obedient subjects."

Barré was very much in the minority, though. In the minds of most members of Parliament, exasperation with the recalcitrant Americans rankled and grew. At the same time, the Americans, encouraged by the success of their resistance to three British tax laws in a row, became increasingly emboldened to resist further forays against their independence.

With all British revenue taxes except that on tea removed, in 1770, the non-importation agreements among the colonists collapsed. And, for the following three years, Americans were grateful to be able to buy all the British goods they wanted, sell their raw materials in return, and try to forget that they had had serious run-ins with British officials.

Many of the colonists, particularly in Massachusetts, even drank a lot of legally imported tea, seemingly able, after the long drought, to swallow the tax of three pence per pound without difficulty. Such was the fondness of the people of Massachusetts for this cheering drink that one of their most eloquent lawyers, James Otis, declared "they would part with all their liberties, and religion too, rather than renounce it." But from the British point of view, far too many Americans kept on drinking illegal tea, smuggled from Holland by way of the Dutch West Indies. In New York City, it was said, the bold smugglers "carted it about at noon day." Customs inspectors were far too few to curb the illegal trade, and too poorly paid to try hard; in fact, some took bribes to ignore it.

However, smuggling, especially in the provinces of New York, Pennsylvania, and Rhode Island, made serious inroads in the East India Company's American tea market. At the same time, widespread smuggling of tea into Britain from Europe greatly diminished the domestic market. So, by February, 1773, the East India Company, the largest commercial enterprise in the Empire, with a legal monopoly of all imports from east of the Cape of Good Hope, had a stifling surplus of tea in its warehouses and was at the edge of bankruptcy. Reckless and inefficient management had added to its woes, as had a sudden national economic recession. The company couldn't even pay its taxes, and the Bank of England wouldn't lend it any more money until it had repaid past loans.

In desperation, the East India directors appealed for help to the King's latest ministry, headed by Lord Frederick North, who took office in 1772. Specifically, they asked for a loan of a million and a half pounds, and permission to sell their surplus tea direct to the Americans, without having to pay the customary import duties either at home or in the colonies. Abolition of the import duties would enable the East India Company to sell its tea for much less than before. By substituting direct sale for the traditional semi-annual tea auctions in London, the company could further reduce the cost of marketing tea in the colonies, probably undercutting the smugglers and putting them to rout. Or, so the hopeful argument ran.

By the time this petition was formally presented to Parliament, the stipulation that the colonial import duty be dropped had somehow disappeared from the text. It was said that Lord North had insisted on deleting it. The few friends of America in Parliament raised the issue promptly, however. One of the more plainspoken of them, William Dowdeswell, warned North to his face: "I tell the noble Lord now, if he don't take off the duty, they won't take the tea."

He was right, of course, but Lord North, so like the King in looks and stubbornness, nimbly dodged through the rain of criticism that followed Dowdeswell's remarks.

"It is to no purpose making objections," the Prime Minister finally declared, deciding to cut off further debate. "The King will have it so. The King means to try the question with America." That ended the argument and the scheme was fashioned into law by a pliant Parliament, to a considerable extent paid for by the King, and passed on May 10, 1773, without a division.

The East India Company directors, some of whom had doubted the success of the plan from the start, then proceeded to implement it by such inept means that its failure was assured. Instead of establishing colonial warehouses and inaugurating seasonal auctions there, at which all provincial tea merchants could share in bidding for the commodity, they voted to adopt what seemed to them to be a much simpler, less expensive, more efficient arrangement. They decided to select just a few regular importers, of established financial responsibility and known loyalty to the Crown, in each of the principal colonial cities: Boston, New York, Philadelphia, and Charleston. To them, the company would consign all the tea expected to be marketed in each region; the consignees were then to share it equally among themselves.

It is curious, to say the least, that, quite apart from the prickly matter of taxation, the East India Company directors apparently gave no thought to how all the other American tea importers—those many scores of wholesalers who had been accustomed to sharing in the business—might react to this sudden, blatant establishment of a monopoly, snatching from all but a tiny few the chance to make any more money in tea. It wouldn't have required much imagination to suspect that when word of the plan reached the colonies, it would immediately alienate all members of the trade except the chosen consignees. An even modestly perceptive man might have foreseen, furthermore, that the scheme would ignite suspicion among all other American businessmen that what the British government and the East India Company had connived to do with the tea trade they might be plotting to do with other lines of commerce between the mother country and the colonies.

Most significantly, the new tea-marketing scheme all but compelled the linking of those Americans whose profits it threatened with those much less conservative citizens whose principles it offended. That made a formidable combination, and it doomed the scheme from the beginning. All that remained to be seen was how the colonies would go about defeating it.

[Benjamin Franklin foreshadowed the reaction of the more vigilant colonial guardians of American rights. Referring to Parliament's Tea Act in a letter written from London to his old friend Thomas Cushing in Boston, less than a month after its passage, Franklin commented sardonically, "They have no idea that any people can act from any principle but that of [self-] interest, and they believe that 3d. in a pound of tea, of which one does not drink perhaps ten lb. in a year, is sufficient to overcome all the patriotism of an American."]

III

Meanwhile, the East India Company's directors proceeded with the task of selecting consignees for the tea. For Boston, William Palmer, one of the leading tea merchants of London, suggested to them the two elder sons of Governor Hutchinson: Thomas, Jr., thirty-three, and Elisha, twenty-seven. Palmer assured the directors that he personally would underwrite their financial obligations to the company. Palmer was an old friend of the Governor, who was a silent partner in the

importing firm his sons ran. Brook Watson, also an eminent London
merchant banker, a one-legged ex-sailor who would one day become
Lord Mayor, proposed two other Bostonians, also business partners,
and guaranteed to furnish bond for them. They were Benjamin
Faneuil, Jr., thirty-two, inheritor of a large fortune accumulated by
his uncle Peter (who had given Faneuil Hall to Boston); and Joshua
Winslow, thirty-six. Winslow, a great-grandson of Governor Edward
Winslow, of the early Plymouth Colony, was a member of a prosperous
family of merchants and ship owners. He was also a cousin of the
Clarke sons.

Jonathan Clarke had arrived in London in late June. He quickly
found out about the new tea-marketing arrangements in prospect,
and, as any other aggressive loyalist businessman would probably have
done, he moved at once to try to obtain part of the Boston allotment
of tea for his own firm.

In a letter to the East India directors, dated July 1st, he wrote:

> GENTLEMEN:
>
> I intended to have made a purchase of teas at your present sale
> to have exported to America, but the candid intimation given by
> you of an intention to export them to the Colonies on account of
> the Company renders it disadvantageous for a single house to
> engage in that article.
>
> I now beg leave, gentlemen, to make a tender to you of the
> services of a house in which I am a partner, Richard Clarke and
> Sons, of Boston, New England, to conduct the sale of such teas
> as you may send to that part of America, in conjunction with any
> other houses you may think proper to entrust with this concern.
> Altho' I have not the honor of being personally known to many
> of you, I flatter myself our house is known to the principal
> merchants who deal to our Province, and are known to have
> always fulfilled our engagements with punctuality & honor, and
> trust I shall procure you ample security for our conducting this
> business, agreeable to the direction we may . . . receive from you.
>
> In soliciting this favor, I beg leave to avail myself further of
> the circumstance of our having for a long time been concerned
> in the tea trade, and to a greater extent than any house in our
> Province, with one exception [the Hutchinson firm] . . . . And

give me leave to add my assurances that the interest of the East
India Company will always be attended to by the house of Richard
Clarke & Sons, if you think fit to repose this confidence in them.

I am, very respectfully, gentlemen,

Your most obed't & humble servant,

Jonathan Clarke

Clarke enclosed two letters of recommendation from London
merchants. He then set out to find a banker willing to put up security
for his firm in case it were awarded a consignment of tea. He was able
to persuade Abraham Dupuis, of Gracechurch Street, to provide the
requisite financial backing—in return for a rather exorbitant commission of one-third of the Clarkes' net commission on sales; to be
hiked to a usurious one-half if other consignments followed.

The two men discussed the terms the Clarkes should propose to the
East India Company, and on the following day Jonathan addressed
another letter to the Honorable Directors:

> If it should be agreeable to you to consign to the house of
> Richard Clarke & Sons, of Boston, New England, this summer
> or fall, I would beg leave to propose to you that I will find security
> to the amount of two or three hundred chests, that in eight
> months after the sale of them in America [the East India Company
> greatly shortened this time span in the final arrangements] the
> accounts shall be forwarded you, and the money for the net
> proceeds paid to your order within that time, you allowing
> our house five per cent commission on the sales, and one per cent
> for storage and other charges, the freight and American duty to
> be chargeable on the teas besides, & we to be free from the risk
> of fire or any other accident that may occur before the delivery
> of the tea.

[Did Jonathan Clarke seriously anticipate "any other accident that
may occur before the delivery of the tea," or was this merely a routine
precaution? There is no clue in the documentation that survives.
There is evidence, however, that at least some of the other gentlemen
involving themselves in the developing tea venture had uneasy pre-
monitions. The London firm of Pigou & Booth, in assuring the East

India Company that it would underwrite the performance of the consignees it recommended for Philadelphia, was careful to stipulate that, if the people of Pennsylvania should refuse to pay the duty or buy the tea, its bond was to be considered void. It can be assumed that the backers of the other tea consignees were equally cautious.]

On August 4th, the East India Company directors announced their selection of consignees. Boston's chosen few were the Hutchinsons, Faneuil, Winslow—and, to Jonathan's delight, Richard Clarke & Sons.

The entire consignment for that port was originally set at three hundred full chests, each containing approximately three hundred and twenty pounds of tea. When the time came for loading, though, three hundred and ninety-eight full and half chests—the variation in size dictated by shipping accommodations—went aboard the four vessels picked to share the cargo. This amounted to around one hundred and five thousand pounds of tea, valued at about £11,000. (The figure varies with nearly every source, and ranges from as low as £8,000 to as high as £18,000. In terms of today's American currency, the value of the tea bound for Boston was at least $75,000, and probably a good deal more.)

A grand total of seventeen hundred full chests, or five hundred and forty-four thousand pounds of tea, was what was first decided upon for the four main ports of entry in the American colonies. That total was finally raised to two thousand chests before the tea ships actually departed for their respective destinations.

The slow, small, square-rigged trading vessels of that day most of which had decks only sixty to eighty feet long and about twenty feet wide, sometimes took eight weeks or longer to cross the Atlantic from London to Boston. They rarely made the eastward passage in less than four weeks, even when boosted by generally favorable winds. This precluded an exchange of correspondence on the desirability of accepting the tea consignments before a decision had to be reached.

This meant that, of the seven men chosen on August 4th to share, ostensibly, all the future tea trade of the Province of Massachusetts Bay, which then included Maine, none except Jonathan Clarke knew about it at the time. The Hutchinsons, Faneuil, and Winslow were not aware that they had become tea consignees of the East India Company until the cargoes were well on their way. They doubtless would have seized the opportunity, though, if their London sponsors hadn't done it for them, and there is no evidence that Richard and Isaac Winslow Clarke were less than pleased when they finally received Jonathan's proud news of his coup.

Jonathan assured the East India Company, in a letter written August 5th, that he would immediately notify his partners in Boston of their selection as consignees. That promised communication undoubtedly explained the terms that the company and the representatives of the tea consignees had agreed upon, and it reached Boston before Jonathan did. The letter could have been sent on his own firm's brig *William,* then loading at a London dock, but Jonathan was too well aware of *William's* sluggish sailing qualities. The brig would do very well to haul part of the tea, but he chose a faster vessel to carry his mail.

At the end of Jonathan's note of August 5th to the East India directors, he scribbled the information that *William,* commanded by Captain Joseph Royal Loring, would be ready to sail in about five days. When the two-master at last weighed anchor and floated down the Thames, it carried fifty-eight chests of tea and a cargo of street lamps, the first ever ordered for Boston.

The terms finally agreed upon for handling the tea consignments were these: each consignee was to receive a gross commission of six per cent on sales; each was to make a deposit of one-eighth of the value of his portion of the consignment immediately and forward the balance within two months after receiving the tea. The deposits naturally had to be advanced by the underwriters in London, thus placing the consignees under specific financial obligations before the tea cargoes ever reached their destinations—a fact which became a major cause for concern to the consignees when the fate of the cargoes became questionable at Boston.

Prices were set at two shillings per pound for Bohea, by far the most popular variety in America (smuggled Bohea was then bringing two shillings, seven pence, per pound in New York), and ranged up to five shillings per pound for green Hyson, the finest variety. These were bargain prices for the time.

The tea consignees were instructed to pay the import tax as unobtrusively as possible, preferably after the tea was sold, and then by bills of exchange on the East India Company, so that it would

seem as if the tax were being paid in London. This they were advised
to do if they could persuade the Commissioners of Customs to accept
that procedure.

The customs men, for their part, were told to be agreeable before
the occasion arose. Their chief, John Robinson, Secretary to the
Treasury, wrote them from London on August 23rd, instructing them
to cooperate fully with the consignees once the tea cargoes arrived.

The day after the East India Company announced its choice of
consignees, it began querying the principal shipping agents in London
for suitable vessels—"constant traders" were stipulated—to carry the
tea to its respective American destinations.

The firm of Lane, Son & Fraser replied at once, stating that the ship
Eleanor, under command of Captain James Bruce, was ready to receive
freight for Boston. *Eleanor*, a three-master of two hundred and fifty
tons, belonged to John Rowe, a plump, amiable, middle-aged ship
owner and merchant, adept at fence-straddling. Rowe endeavored to
be on friendly terms with everybody in Boston, whatever his politics
might be, and largely succeeded. He attended all the best Whig parties,
but regularly went perch-fishing with John Montagu, the British
admiral stationed at Boston.

Rowe also gave his ship captains a free hand in soliciting cargoes
abroad. In this case, by accepting some of the East India Company's
tea, Captain Bruce, a man of Loyalist sympathies, would cause his
employer anguished embarrassment.

One shipping agent solicited was George Hayley, the London
partner of John Hancock, elegant young lightweight figurehead and
chief financial backer of Boston's Sons of Liberty. Hayley was an
aggressive businessman and an alert garnerer of cargoes, but in this
instance discretion overcame his acquisitive instinct. He deliberately
delayed replying to East India House for five days, presumably so
that Hancock's only vessel in port, the 150-ton three-master *Hayley*,
could finish loading. Only then did he report, with a comfortable
conscience, that the *Hayley* was "now ready to sail," and thus unable
to take on any of the tea. (The fate of the Boston tea ships might have
been quite different if one of them had belonged to John Hancock.
This was a near miss.) Hayley said he expected to dispatch the ship by
August 15th.

Rather than give an entirely negative reply to the East India people,

Hayley called their attention to the year-old *Dartmouth*, another three-masted constant trader, also out of Boston. *Dartmouth* was expected to head homeward from London in "about 14 days." This vessel, under the command of Captain James Hall, was owned principally by three Quaker brothers from New Bedford named Rotch.

Within the following several weeks, the East India Company's staff arranged for one hundred and fourteen chests of the Boston-bound tea to go aboard the *Eleanor,* another one hundred and fourteen aboard the *Dartmouth,* and one hundred and twelve aboard the brig *Beaver,* which, like *Dartmouth,* belonged to the Rotches. Charleston's tea was stowed in the hold of the *London,* Philadelphia's went aboard the *Polly,* and New York's was loaded on the *Nancy.* These were all larger vessels than those headed for Boston.

The tea ships left one by one, the last clearing London by early October, but all of them—and *Hayley,* too, on which Jonathan Clarke had taken passage home—were variously held up for weeks by autumnal headwinds. The adverse winds kept them sheltering in harbors along the Strait of Dover before they ventured out upon the storm-whipped Atlantic.

While the forcibly idled men aboard these ships fretted away their time, they kept up with the London newspapers as best they could. Ship captains had standing orders to bring the latest news back with them for reprinting in the provincial press. The most recent London newspaper that Captain Scott carried with him when *Hayley* finally dropped down the Channel was dated September 24th. An earlier issue, also aboard the *Hayley,* contained an item that must have given Jonathan Clarke some troubled thoughts. It read:

> A Merchant, trading to America, hath offered a bet of ten guineas to five that not a pound of the teas now sending out by the India Company to Boston, New-York, and Pennsylvania will ever reach those markets, that some ACCIDENT will HAPPEN TO IT— either the ship's bottom will spring a leak in the harbour, or the tea will by some ACCIDENT or other take fire after it is landed, and be lost that way.

IV

On the morning of November 2nd, none of the tea ships had yet
reached Boston, nor would *Hayley* bring Jonathan Clarke home for
another fortnight, yet none of the men to whom those peremptory
messages from "O.C." had been delivered was any longer in ignorance
of the East India Company's scheme or of his own involuntary part
in it. Whether or not any informative personal letters had yet reached
them from London is not known, but all of Boston found out on
October 18th what was afoot and who was involved.

On that morning, the Boston *Gazette and Country Journal*, a
weekly that appeared on Mondays and was the principal organ of the
Sons of Liberty, revealed the gist of the plan "destructive to the
happiness of every well-wisher to his country." The story ran:

> It is the current Talk of the Town that Richard Clarke,
> Benjamin Faneuil, and the two young Messers Hutchinson are
> appointed to receive the Tea allowed to be exported for this
> place. This new Scheme of Administration, lately *said* to be *so
> friendly* to the Colonies, is at once so threatening to the trade,
> and so well calculated to establish and encrease [sic] the detested
> TRIBUTE, that an attempt to meddle with this pernicious Drug
> would render men much more respected than they are as ob-
> noxious as were the Commissioners of stampt paper in 1765.
>
> Should the Tea now shipping for Boston be returned to
> England, as it undoubtedly will, if the People do not insist on
> copying the resolutions of Philadelphia and New-York to destroy
> it, Lord North will meet with a rebuff, which will put his utmost
> firmness to the Trial. It will be impossible for his Lordship after
> having exerted all his cunning in flattering the East India Com-
> pany to withstand their peremptory demand of a total repeal of
> the Tea Act.
>
> A correspondent has hinted that it would be highly improper
> to return those great Cargoes of Tea that are expected without
> sending the important Gentlemen whose existence depends on it
> along with it, to give the Premier the reasons for such conduct.

This was the first direct warning to the tea consignees (though
Winslow's name, oddly, was omitted), and the mildest, to appear in
the *Gazette*, to which Samuel Adams, James Otis, Doctor Joseph

Warren, John Adams, and other well-known Boston Whigs regularly contributed.

It was followed a week later by much heavier fire. This took the form of a reprint of a handbill that had been circulated first in Philadelphia and then reprinted in the newspapers of that city and of New York. It was an open letter to all the tea consignees appointed for the colonies, and it was signed SCAEVOLA, a name of symbolic significance to the classically educated newspaper readers of that day, for Scaevola was a hero of the early Roman republic, a paragon of steadfastness in the face of acute peril.

The open letter, in part, read:

> GENTLEMEN:
>
> Your appointment . . . justly claims the attention of every man who wishes well to this country. And you need not be surprised to find the eyes of ALL now fixed on you, as on men who have it in their power to ward off the most dangerous stroke that has been ever meditated against the liberties of America.
>
> You have before you the examples of many of your unhappy countrymen; I mean *some* of the STAMP MASTERS; examples which, if properly attended to, may convince you how foolish, how *dangerous*, it is to undertake to force the loathsome pills of slavery and oppression down the throats of a free, independent, and *determined* people. Your appointment is exactly similar to that of our late STAMP MASTERS: They were commissioned to enforce one revenue act; you, to execute another. The Stamp and Tea Laws were both designed to raise a revenue and to establish *parliamentary despotism* in America. . . .
>
> You cannot believe that the Tea Act, with respect to its design and tendency, differs in one single point from the Stamp Act. If there be any difference, the *Tea Act is the more dangerous*. The Stamp Act was sensibly felt by all ranks of people, and was therefore opposed by all, but the Tea Act, more insidious in its operation, required some pains to discover its malignity. Under the first [Act] no man could transfer his property; he could not even read a newspaper; without seeing and feeling the detestable imposition; it was therefore too glaring to pass unnoticed and unopposed. But, under the Tea Law, the duty, being paid on importation, is afterwards laid on the article, and becomes so

blended with the price of it that, although every man who purchases tea imported from Britain must of course pay the duty, yet every man does not know it, and may, therefore, not object to it. It is in vain, then, to seek for any distinction between the two employments. To Americans, it must be a matter of indifference by what style or title you may think proper to demean yourselves: whether STAMP MASTERS or TEA COMMISSIONERS. If you are appointed to enforce the revenue act in America, any titles you may assume to yourselves in the execution of your office will prove DETESTABLE and INFAMOUS.

If Parliament can of right tax us 10 pounds for any purpose, they may of right tax us 10,000, and so on, without end. And if we allow them a fair opportunity of pleading precedent by a successful execution of the Tea Act, under *your* auspices, we may bid adieu to all that is dear and valuable amongst men. . . . You are marked out as political bombardiers to demolish the fair structure of American liberty, and much, very much, depends on your conduct at this time. . . .

There was much, very much more, enough to fill most of two columns of an inside page of the *Gazette*.

By the following Monday, November 1st, the attack on the tea consignees had warmed to the extent that the *Gazette* devoted its entire front page, except for a scattering of small ads, to the growing controversy. The *Gazette* was only one of several Boston newspapers at the time, but it was the best and had the widest audience. Richard Clarke had been a regular advertiser in the *Gazette* as recently as August, and probably still read it, however much it must have angered him. In any event, there can be no doubt that the tea consignees in Boston were thoroughly aware of the strong, spreading opposition to their roles by the time they were roused from their beds in the small hours of November 2nd to receive their respective summonses to confront that opposition, for the first time, under the Liberty Tree on the following day.

V

The core of the opposition was a small, secret group representing the most militant element of the Sons of Liberty. They called themselves the "Loyal Nine." They were pledged not to reveal anything they did to any outsider who didn't have their complete trust. From at least as early as the summer of 1765 they had been the activists who plotted and helped carry out most anti-British demonstrations in Boston.

Their regular meeting place was a small room, which they called Liberty Hall, on the second floor of Chase & Speakman's distillery. That rum manufactory stood on Hanover Square, near the Liberty Tree. Thomas Chase, of the firm, was a member of the Loyal Nine. So was Henry Bass, an admiring young merchant cousin of Samuel Adams. The other members were John Avery, Jr., a distiller, son-in-law of Thomas Cushing, Speaker of the Massachusetts House of Representatives; Stephen Cleverly, a brazier; Thomas Crafts, a painter; Benjamin Edes, a printer and member of the firm of Edes & Gill, publishers of the *Gazette*; John Smith, a brazier; George Trott, a jeweler; and Henry Welles, whose profession is not known.

They were a group of ardent young Whigs, and their leader, according to his principal biographer, was Samuel Adams. Adams, though not actually a member of the Loyal Nine, was their warm friend and constant adviser.

[It was the Loyal Nine who fashioned an effigy of Andrew Oliver and hung it from the Liberty Tree in the middle of an August night in 1765, when the town was in a fury over the Stamp Act and Oliver had been named stamp master for Boston. It was they who next evening turned loose the former South End gang of waterfront toughs, led by Ebenezer Mackintosh, a cobbler, to destroy a building thought to be intended for Oliver's headquarters, and then cut down his effigy from the Liberty Tree, parade it through the streets, and ceremoniously behead it in front of his house. Later that evening, Mackintosh's mob returned, encouraged by rum, and smashed all the windows of the Oliver residence. Several rioters burst into the house and tried to find the owner, yelling that they would kill him. Forewarned by his brother-in-law Thomas Hutchinson, then Lieutenant-Governor, Oliver had slipped away.

Two weeks later, the Loyal Nine once again unleashed Mackintosh and his "chickens," as he called them, this time to bully Hutchinson. It was a thrust that was badly bungled. Samuel Adams and others had spread the falsehood that Hutchinson had conspired with British officials to devise the Stamp Act. In truth, he had strongly advised them against it. Once it had become law, however, he felt obligated to enforce it to the limit of his ability. Hutchinson had an almost obsessive sense of duty, and it was responsible for a good deal of his unpopularity.

That night, Mackintosh's gang got entirely out of hand, and in a drunken frenzy stripped Hutchinson's house to its bare wood. The Lieutenant-Governor heard them roaring up the street and escaped down back alleys before they arrived. They wrecked his wine cellar, stole all his household money, clothes, and furnishings, and strewed the muddy streets with the precious source material and manuscript pages of his distinguished *History of the Colony and Province of Massachusetts Bay*. When the rioters were finally called off, they had even begun to remove all the paneling in the house and to dismantle the roof.

The next day, in court, Hutchinson swore, with tears in his eyes, that he had been in no way responsible for the passage of the Stamp Act. He declared that what had been done to his property the night before was "the most barbarous outrage which ever was committed in America." A great many respectable citizens of Boston agreed with him, and voted their compassionate apologies at the next town meeting. Hutchinson always claimed that some of the rioters were among those who voted to compensate him for the senseless damage.

It became obvious to Samuel Adams and the Loyal Nine at this point that excessive violence in the cause of colonial liberties might create martyrs rather than win followers. From then on, except in the shameful instance of the Boston Massacre, in 1770, Mackintosh's mob became noticeably more disciplined, even marching in military formation at public celebrations. By 1773, it could be counted on to misbehave only within carefully calculated limits.

The attack on Andrew Oliver in August, 1765, had led him to promise the next day to resign his appointment as stamp master, but four months later he still had not brought himself to do so.

It was then, in mid-December, 1765, that the Loyal Nine decided to act again. Composing a summons worded almost precisely like those sent to the tea consignees eight years later, they ordered Oliver to appear at the Liberty Tree at noon on Tuesday, December 17th, and publicly resign his commission. After midnight on Sunday, Benjamin Edes printed a hundred copies of an announcement to the people of Boston to assemble on Tuesday noon and witness Oliver's resignation. Between 9 a.m. and 3 p.m. on Monday, the announcements were pasted up all over town, doubtless by boys hired for the purpose.

The plot worked to perfection. Oliver was escorted to the scene of his humiliation on December 17th by Ebenezer Mackintosh, but with suitable decorum. There was no misbehavior, just barely restrained hostility.

We know of the Loyal Nine's part in this escapade because Henry Bass couldn't resist sharing the fun with his intended father-in-law, Samuel Phillips Savage, a former Boston selectman then living in Weston. Bass wrote Savage a letter two days after Oliver's resignation, describing the mechanics of the plot but urging Savage to "keep this a profound Secret." Savage, nevertheless, saved the letter. Bass had added, in a postscript, "We do every thing in order to keep this & the first Affair [the raid on Oliver's house? on Hutchinson's?] Private, and are not a little pleas'd to hear that McIntosh has the Credit of the whole Affair."

Savage was not the only sympathetic and trusted outsider to be let in on the secret. On the very day that Bass wrote to Savage, John Adams noted in his diary that "Messrs. Crafts and Chase [both members of the Loyal Nine] gave me a particular account of the proceedings of the Sons of Liberty on Tuesday last." He perhaps didn't know the inner group's secret name. A month later, when he was invited to spend a social evening with the "Sons of Liberty," and recorded their names in his diary, he listed all members of the Loyal Nine except Henry Welles, who was absent. Joseph Field, a ship's captain, and Adams were the only guests. Adams reported that he "was very civilly and respectfully treated by all present. We had punch, wine, pipes and tobacco, biscuit and cheese, etc. I heard nothing but such conversation as passes at all clubs, among gentlemen, about the times." With irony, he concluded, "No plots, no machinations."]

John Adams ten years after the Tea Party, as Copley painted him in London during negotiations leading to the signing of a peace treaty with Great Britain.

The "secretary" of the Loyal Nine was John Avery, Jr., probably chosen for the role because he was the best-educated member. Avery was a graduate of Harvard, as his father and grandfather had been. Doctor Joseph Warren was one of his classmates.

Why Avery chose to use the signature "M.Y., *Sec'y*" for the early manifestoes of the Loyal Nine, but switched to "O.C., *Sec'y*" for those sent to the tea consignees, is not clear. They were doubtless random choices, dictated only by the need to avoid using the actual initials of anyone the group knew.

VI

Of the seven men who became the Loyal Nine's special targets in the fall of 1773, Richard Clarke was by far the oldest, but age mattered little in a group of individuals linked by so many ties. They were all graduates of Harvard and large-scale importers, especially of tea. Their families, long prominent in the political and commercial affairs of the Province of Massachusetts Bay, had widely intermarried. Their connections with the leading officials of the Province were close. Thomas and Elisha Hutchinson were not only sons of the Governor but nephews of the Lieutenant-Governor, Andrew Oliver. The latter's brother, Peter, was Chief Justice, and he had married Richard Clarke's sister. Governor Hutchinson is said to have been Richard Clarke's uncle, which is genealogically conceivable but seems improbable, since both men were the same age, sixty-two. Also, Hutchinson once referred to Clarke in a private letter as "old Mr. Clarke," an odd choice of descriptive phrase for either one's nephew or one's exact contemporary.

The Clarke confreres and their family connections represented the most conservative element among those rather numerous Massachusetts citizens who in 1773 felt no urge to alter the imperial relationship between the Province and Great Britain. The associates shared a singular insensitivity to popular sentiment, and an incredible narrowness of viewpoint. They appear to have failed to appreciate how their joint venture in tea would alienate their normally friendly business competitors and drive them to combine forces, however uneasily, with political radicals to spoil the associates' plans. At no time did they seem to comprehend why what was simply an attractive busi-

John Singleton Copley painted this charming group portrait of himself, family, and father-in-law, Richard Clarke, in London during the summer of 1776.

ness proposition to them appeared to be nothing less than a menacing, subversive plot both to those who disagreed with them politically and those who comprised the majority of their business community.

In the Boston tea consignees' eagerness to gain from this immensely unpopular enterprise, they brought upon themselves, their city, and, in short order, their country a crisis that they obviously hadn't foreseen and whose magnitude they probably couldn't even have imagined.

Their instinctive reaction to challenges from the Sons of Liberty, who they thought behaved like a revolutionary tribunal, was outraged and contemptuous defiance. Their attitude was made all the more stubborn by their knowledge that the law, the power of the King's government, and the convictions of the people whose opinions they valued confirmed them in their stand. Most of all, they felt fortified against mounting public pressure by the encouragement— indeed, the self-righteous insistence—of Governor Hutchinson.

It is frustrating not to be able to see these mistaken tea consignees more clearly across the years. After playing their brief, incidental roles in hastening the outbreak of the American Revolution, their personal histories were lost in the rush of much more important events. We can't even study the faces of any of them today except Richard Clarke. Portraits of the others are not known to exist, but that of the elder Clarke is symbolic of the spirit displayed by them all.

[Clarke had a naturally defiant look, as one can see in the National Gallery of Art in Washington, where it is captured forever in an engaging family portrait painted in 1776 by his celebrated son-in-law John Singleton Copley. That great American artist included Clarke in the large painting because by then the older man was making his home with the Copleys and their four small children in London, having felt obliged to flee there from Boston, shorn of most of his fortune, in December, 1774.

We know that Copley, as usual, had achieved "a very striking likeness" of every individual on the wide canvas, for Samuel Curwen, a longtime family friend and fellow-exile who had been Judge of Admiralty at Boston, dropped in for tea when the portrait was nearly finished, and recorded that enthusiastic opinion in his diary.

Richard Clarke sits there proudly, ignoring the small granddaughter on his lap, who is reaching her arms appealingly toward his neck. His head is high, his blue eyes clear and calm, his mouth set firmly. He

Thomas Hutchinson, Royal Governor of the Province of Massachusetts Bay, painted perhaps in early middle age. He always looked younger than he was.

stares into the distance with an air of such obvious self-assurance that it is easy to believe that he hadn't the faintest doubt that his course back home had been correct, despite its disastrous effect upon his personal circumstances, and that the Sons of Liberty would live to regret their headstrong behavior.]

The imperious knocks on Richard Clarke's front door in Boston early that November morning in 1773 signaled the beginning of a historic drama, in much the way that the eighteenth-century stage director's raps on the floor with his ceremonial staff traditionally heralded the commencement of plays. Its climax occurred a month and a half later, in that seriocomic incident called the Boston Tea Party, which, though surely the quietest and most orderly mob action on record in America, led directly, through its consequences, to the initial armed clashes of the Revolution.

VII

Essentially, the opposing sides in the angry controversy developing in Boston over the impending tea polarized around two men who had been enemies for years: Thomas Hutchinson and Samuel Adams.

Hutchinson inevitably loomed large in the controversy, since he represented the openly defied royal government. Adams, as always, shunned conspicuousness, preferring to plot the course of anti-royalist events and inspire the appropriate propaganda in secret.

A master politician and a propagandist of genius, Adams had been working designedly since 1768, he admitted in later years, to bring about the complete independence of the American colonies. Those whom he manipulated to help implement his plans—John Hancock, for one—were not always conscious of the manipulation or ready to admit that they would like to accomplish the same goal. But Adams had great patience, a sustaining vision, and inflexible determination. In the last quality, he found his match in Thomas Hutchinson.

Hutchinson, though his great-great-grandmother Anne had been banished from the Plymouth Colony as a rebel and a heretic, was an instinctive aristocrat. He believed that loyalty to the King was the highest form of patriotism. He was a man of unquestioned integrity, whose chief disadvantage was a narrowness of viewpoint combined

Samuel Adams, in an appropriately declamatory pose, was painted by Copley some time between 1770 and 1772, at the request and expense of John Hancock.

with an almost religious devotion to consistency. He was also a scholar, with a sound background in Latin, fluency in French, and considerable talent as a writer of history. John Adams once wrote, moreover, that Thomas Hutchinson had the best mind for finance that he had ever known. Probably because of that ability, which had made him a fortune, Hutchinson tended to regard with varying degrees of condescension those who had done less well financially than he had.

Yet he was not altogether an unlikable man; quite the contrary. Back in 1763, before the Boston *Gazette* became his persistent gadfly, that newspaper had once described him as "a tall, slender, fair-complexioned, fair-spoken, very good gentleman," who had "captivated half the pretty Ladies in the colony" and won the approval of "more than half the pretty Gentlemen." Even at the age of sixty-two, in 1773, he was still a slim, elegant figure, the very model of a royal governor.

Samuel Adams was as instinctively a populist as Hutchinson was an aristocrat, and also looked and lived the part.

Their personal antagonism began on Adams' side. More than thirty years before the events described in this narrative, Thomas Hutchinson and his father, unswerving advocates of sound-money policies, had helped persuade Parliament to dissolve the inflationary Massachusetts Land Bank, of which Deacon Adams, Sam's father, was the principal advocate. In consequence, Deacon Adams lost nearly all his money, a fact that his son, not yet through Harvard at the time, very naturally resented and blamed entirely on the Hutchinsons.

After Deacon Adams died, Sam, who had no head for money or any fondness for it, soon squandered the few pounds his father had managed to leave him, and let the small family brewery go to ruin. How he managed to support a house, a wife, two children, a black slave girl, and a Newfoundland dog was a mystery to many of his contemporaries, and largely remains one still. Samuel Adams had a host of friends, however, and some of the more affluent, including Hancock, helped keep him afloat.

Despite his puritanical austerity and a frugality both natural and obligatory, Sam was liked by people of all levels of society in Boston. This helped him obtain a variety of bureaucratic jobs. Even when he was dramatically in arrears as Boston's tax collector, because he didn't have the heart to put pressure on delinquent taxpayers (especially if they had a reasonable excuse), he was reelected by a substantial margin.

Adams' real power lay in his intuitive and inspired grasp of the science of politics, of which he was an undoubted master, and in his brilliant flair for propaganda. His polemic production, printed mostly in the *Gazette*, was voluminous and highly effective. His correspondence, with like-minded men throughout the colonies as well as in Massachusetts, was astoundingly large and compelling. His active and clever pen more than made up for the fact that in appearance he was invariably seedy and looked much older than he was—fifty-one in 1773; and that his hands trembled and his voice quavered with palsy.

As the pre-Revolutionary years went by, Adams became increasingly active in fighting the royal government and its attempts to encroach upon American liberties. Hutchinson, who had scarcely been aware of him as an individual at the time of the Land Bank debacle, came to focus suspicion and hostility upon Sam Adams as the source of all his administrative troubles—which was substantially true. Hutchinson, in fact, became almost obsessive in suspecting the hand of Sam Adams in every obstructive act of his constituents.

"I doubt," he once wrote, "whether there is a greater Incendiary in the King's dominions or a man of greater malignity of heart, or who less scruples any measure ever so criminal to accomplish his purpose; and I think I do him no injustice when I suppose he wishes the destruction of every Friend to Government in America."

The hatred was fully reciprocated. Adams never had a kind or respectful word for the Governor, and on at least one occasion referred to him as "that fiend Hutchinson."

Brickbats and Paper Skirmishes

(November 3 — December 16, 1773)

I

A LL the bells of Boston began ringing at eleven o'clock in the morning of Wednesday, November 3rd, while at the same time the town crier started on his rounds through the cobbled streets, issuing singsong public invitations to gather at the Liberty Tree by noon.

Already, most of the tea consignees had made their way to Richard Clarke & Sons' warehouse, near the foot of King Street, and were conferring in the counting room, at the top of a narrow flight of stairs. With them were about two dozen of their more rugged friends, offering reassurance, and ready to provide physical support in case of need. At least one of them was a man of authority: Nathaniel Hatch, a judge of the Inferior Court of the Province and a justice of the peace for Suffolk County, of which Boston was the seat.

Elisha Hutchinson was missing. The weak excuse given was that he must somehow have misunderstood the plan of action, though it was simple enough—"to oppose the designs of the mob, if they should come to offer us any insult or injury," as Richard Clarke later expressed it. But Elisha's brother Tom was there, declaring that he would act for both.

Jonathan Clarke was still out on the Atlantic, of course, with two weeks of rough voyaging ahead of him before he reached home.

So, in all, five of the seven men chosen to market the East India Company's tea in Boston henceforth were present. Joshua Winslow, only recently returned from a business trip to Nova Scotia, was there reluctantly, for he was in declining health.

31

Dr. Joseph Warren, popular Boston physician and advocate of American independence, as Copley painted him not long before the Tea Party.

"You may well judge that none of us ever entertained the least thoughts of obeying the summons sent us to attend at Liberty Tree," Richard Clarke assured Abraham Dupuis, his London underwriter, in a subsequent letter describing the situation. "And on this occasion we were so happy as to be supported by a number of gentlemen of the first rank."

This, in Clarke's mind at least, was in gratifying contrast to the complexion of the crowd of some five hundred persons that had gathered under the Liberty Tree by midday. "They consisted chiefly of people of the lowest rank," or so he said he had been told. "Very few reputable tradesmen, as we are informed, appeared amongst them. There were indeed two merchants, reputed rich, and the selectmen of the town, but these last say they went to prevent disorder."

There was no disorder to prevent at Liberty Tree, but it soon developed elsewhere.

By one o'clock, the crowd had become impatient over the failure of the summoned tea consignees to appear, and many of them had set out to find the reason for it.

The uneasy group waiting in Clarkes' counting room saw them coming down King Street, and watched tensely as they swarmed to a halt outside, making way for a delegation of nine to approach the warehouse. A servant opened the double door for this committee, which tramped grimly up the stairs to the counting room.

All the men of the committee were known to the assembled tea consignees and their friends—though, with a couple of exceptions, not favorably. The principal exception was Dr. Joseph Warren (who was to die heroically at the Battle of Bunker Hill only a year and a half later). Warren, an ardent Whig, able orator, and close friend of John Adams, was Boston's most popular physician, although true his popularity depended to some degree on one's political viewpoint. To Henry Hulton, one of the British customs officials at Boston, Warren was "that rascally apothecary."

A serene-browed, very blond young man, then thirty-two years old, with an easy charm and infectious lightheartedness, Warren had the reputation of being a dedicated, sympathetic doctor, methodically clean—a rarity in those days. He had been at Harvard with Tom Hutchinson, Ben Faneuil, and Jonathan Clarke, and was on casually friendly terms with them. It may have been somewhat reassuring to Hutchinson and Faneuil to see Warren's friendly face among the unwelcome delegates of the street crowd, yet it more likely was unsettling, for it undermined their complacent conviction that their opponents were all a scurvy lot.

Richard Clarke's indignation at being challenged by the "mob-ility" may have been somewhat mollified by the presence on the committee of William Dennie, one of the town's ship owners. If so, he didn't know his man very well. John Rowe, the cautious Whig who owned the *Eleanor,* had recently seen Dennie, along with Paul Revere and William Molineux, "badly abusing" two British customs officers as they came out of a tavern one evening. Dennie was not likely to be indulgent toward Clarke and his associates, who seemed to be in league with the customs men.

None of the tea consignees could have been much impressed to find Dr. Benjamin Church among their visitors that afternoon. Church, who had topped off his Harvard education with practical experience in London hospitals, was the best-trained doctor in Boston, but he was also a well-known rake. What wasn't then known to anyone but himself in the Clarkes' counting room was that Dr. Church, in a desperate effort to support the extravagances of his mistress and his own expensive tastes, had for a year been a paid informer for General Thomas Gage, commander-in-chief of the British forces in North America. Church was certainly no threat to Clarke and his friends, therefore, but he was indeed a danger to his fellow-committeemen.

Yet neither Warren, Dennie, nor Church was in charge of the delegation now confronting the tea consignees. Instead, the man blusteringly in command was William Molineux, whom John Rowe once labeled in his diary "First Leader in Dirty Matters." Molineux, a hardware merchant in financial straits, was the disappointing and disappointed son of an Irish knight, a prominent surgeon of Dublin. He was irascible and contentious, a trial even to his friends and a particularly insistent goad to his foes, mostly Britishers, his special peeve.

Molineux, dark and furious, strode over to face Richard Clarke.

"From whom are you a committee?" Clarke asked coldly.

"From the whole people," Molineux shouted, in his customary conversational tone, and immediately launched upon a blistering lecture.

"He told us that we had committed an high insult on the people," Clarke afterward described it to Dupuis, "in refusing to give them that most reasonable satisfaction which had been demanded in the summons or notice which had been sent us."

Molineux then read a paper, which he said they must all sign, containing a solemn promise not to unload the expected tea or pay duty on it, and to ship it back to England in the vessels that brought it.

"Which extravagant demand being firmly refused, and treated with proper contempt by all of us," Richard Clarke wrote, "Mr. Molineux then said that since we had refused their most reasonable demands, we must expect to feel, on our first appearance, the utmost weight of the people's resentment."

Molineux then abruptly herded his committee back down to the street. When they rejoined the crowd, several members began shouting, "Out with them! Out with them!" and moved threateningly toward the building. (According to the *Gazette* when it reported the incident, the crowd had originally intended to leave immediately after the delegates returned, but the latter had been "received with such hauteur" that their supporters were stung to retaliation.)

At this point, Richard Clarke sent his servant down at a run to close the warehouse doors. Judge Hatch, already past fifty, and four younger men followed close behind. They reached the doors just as the first wave of attackers reached them.

There was a grunting, shoving struggle, over which Judge Hatch could be heard shouting, "In His Majesty's name, I order you to desist and disperse!" The command lost emphasis, however, because the Judge was trying to help close the doors at the same time, and was short of breath. He was merely jeered and insulted.

Outside pressure on the doors suddenly ceased, but only because, unknown to those inside, the leaders of the crowd had decided to take them off their hinges. Seizing advantage of the brief lull, Judge Hatch and his helpers slammed the doors shut and bolted them, then scrambled upstairs.

Some of the attackers soon had the doors removed, while others surged into the warehouse and made a rush for the stairs. They were met by about twenty of the youngest men from the counting room, who had grabbed up canes, chairs, and whatever else they might use for weapons, and clattered down the steps to blunt the charge.

The battle was vigorous and noisy, but damaging mostly to those in the narrow front ranks, while the crude wooden staircase groaned and threatened to splinter and collapse. After the initial blows and bruises, the determination of the attackers wilted. They made a few half-hearted efforts to rally, but in a short while retreated to the street.

There, for at least an hour and a half, the crowd blockaded the building, taunting those inside to come out.

This maneuver finally palled, and the besiegers began straggling away. When the crowd had thinned noticeably, and seemed no longer formidable, Richard Clarke and his friends decided to leave, in a body. Together they moved up King Street. A few insults were shouted at them, but no one attempted to interfere with their progress. At the top of the street, congratulating themselves on having won at least a temporary victory, they parted company and went to their homes, "without any molestation, saving some insulting behavior from a few despicable persons."

Thursday evening, Benjamin Faneuil found another message from "O.C., *Sec'y,*" lying on the floor of his front hallway. It had obviously been thrust under the door, and it was addressed to all the tea consignees. This time, the tone of the message was vicious. It read:

GENTLEMEN:

It is currently reported that you are in the extremest anxiety respecting your standing with the good people of this Town and Province, as commissioners of the sale of the monopolized and dutied tea. We do not wonder in the least that your apprehensions are terrible, when the most enlightened, humane & conscientious community on the earth view you in the light of tigers or mad dogs, whom the public safety obliges them to destroy. Long have this people been irreconcilable to the idea of spilling human blood, on almost any occasion whatever; but they have lately seen a penitential thief suffer death for pilfering a few pounds from scattering individuals [executions were then public, and the gallows stood beside the town gate on the narrow Neck, the only land approach to Boston]. You boldly avow a resolution to bear a principal part in the robbery of every inhabitant of this country, in the present and future ages, of every thing dear and interesting to them. Are there no laws in the Book of God and nature that enjoin such miscreants to be cut off from among the people, as troublers of the whole congregation?

Yea, verily, there are laws and officers to put them into execution, which you can neither corrupt, intimidate, nor escape, and whose resolution to bring you to condign punishment you can only avoid by a speedy imitation of your brethren in Philadelphia [the tea commissioners there had already submitted to insistent public demand and promised not to land the tea when it arrived]. This people are still averse to precipitate your fate, but in case of much longer delay in complying with their indispensable demands, you will not fail to meet the just rewards of your avarice & insolence.

Remember, gentlemen, this is the last warning you are ever to expect from the insulted, abused, and most indignant vindicators of violated liberty in the Town of Boston.

The missive was dated "Thursday evening, 9 o'clock. Nov. 4, 1773." The Loyal Nine had collaborated on the text, as usual, and perhaps the vengeful tone reflected the lingering sting of cuts and bruises suffered in the fracas at Clarkes' warehouse.

The tea consignees, despite what appeared to be overwhelming odds, didn't scare easily. If anything, their resistance stiffened.

Earlier on Thursday, the selectmen of Boston had issued a notice to the community to attend a special town meeting the next day to discuss this alarming affair. The selectmen had been persuaded to convene the townspeople to give formal expression to the community's sentiments regarding the tea, especially since one of the consignees, and several of their friends, so the *Gazette* reported, had let it be known that if the harassed gentlemen were asked properly, and not brutishly, they would indeed resign—a report evidently without substance.

On Thursday, also, Governor Hutchinson summoned his Council, the small, select upper body of the provincial legislature, to meet with him to determine an official course of action. Hutchinson had no delusions regarding the degree of support he might expect from his Council, the members of which he knew to be predominantly anti-administration, but he felt that it was his duty to make the try. The results of the meeting confirmed his skepticism. The Council merely voted that "the Attorney-General be ordered to prosecute the persons concerned in this riot." But everyone knew in advance that the persons concerned would never be identified.

Describing the clash at the warehouse in a letter to Brook Watson of London, Benjamin Faneuil noted the Council's decision, and concluded sarcastically, "The consequence, I suppose, will be, the grand jury will not find a bill against them [the rioters], and there the affair will end." He proved to be a true prophet.

William Legge, 2nd Earl of Dartmouth, was Secretary of State for the American Department, and thus Governor Hutchinson's superior, at the time of the Tea Party.

Governor Hutchinson, summing up the incident in a weary report on November 4th to his British chief, the Earl of Dartmouth, Secretary of State for the American Department, complained once more that the government of the Province of Massachusetts Bay was effectively being taken out of his hands. The actual government, he said, resided in the Boston town meeting, under the firm control of Samuel Adams.

[Hutchinson repeatedly declared illegal the various mass meetings held in Boston during the tense weeks that followed. His stand was based on the technicality that a Boston town meeting wasn't legitimate if it included voters from other towns. This was always the case that fall, because Samuel Adams' Committee of Correspondence invariably issued urgent invitations to surrounding towns to send delegates to every public meeting of Boston citizens. Adams was determined to give the opposition to the British government's action a province-wide coloration, though even he recognized the legal weight of Hutchinson's attitude. This was evaded by referring to these large multi-community gatherings as meetings of "the body of the people"; Adams didn't pretend that they were Boston town meetings. This seemed all the more irregular to Hutchinson. Furthermore, even if Boston alone had been represented, Hutchinson was set against town meetings that dealt with any but purely parochial matters. He sincerely believed that matters of broader scope were simply not their rightful concern.]

II

An earnest crowd of a thousand persons or more—"perhaps in every regard as respectable as ever assembled in Faneuil Hall," the *Gazette* declared—convened in that favorite meeting place at 10 A.M. on Friday, November 5th, and chose John Hancock for moderator.

The first order of business was to deal with a handbill entitled "Tradesmen's Protest," which had been distributed throughout the hall just before the meeting. It was anonymous, but purported to be a defense of the tea consignees by their fellow-businessmen, who deplored the town's antagonistic treatment of them.

Hancock dealt with this by inviting all present who called themselves tradesmen to move to the south side of the hall. Some four

John Hancock, in an obvious wig, commissioned this Copley portrait of himself to hang beside the one of Samuel Adams in his drawing room on Beacon Hill.

hundred men rapidly collected there. Now, then, he asked, do you gentlemen acknowledge this "Tradesmen's Protest"? They responded with
a vigorous chorus of "No"s. Hancock then declared the Protest to be
"base, false, and scandalous." The handbills were ripped, crumpled,
and forgotten.

The voters then proceeded to appropriate and endorse unanimously
a set of resolves that had been drawn up in mid-October by the citizens
of Philadelphia.

Those resolves, in clearest language, denied the right of Parliament
to tax Americans without their consent, declared it to be the duty of
all to oppose this latest attempt to do so, denounced the avowed purpose of the tax—to support the King's officials, justices, and troops in
America—and excoriated those Americans who would help Parliament
achieve its purpose.

The next-to-last resolve declared, "That whoever shall, directly or
indirectly, countenance this attempt, or in any wise aid or abet in unloading, receiving, or vending the tea sent or to be sent out by the
East India Company, while it remains subject to the payment of a duty
here, is an enemy to America."

The final resolve expressed in courteous terms what the Loyal Nine
had so roughly demanded: "That a committee be immediately chosen
to wait on those gentlemen who, it is reported, are appointed by the
East India Company to receive and sell said tea, and request them,
from a regard to their own characters, and the peace and good order
of this Town and Province, immediately to resign their appointments."

The committee chosen was headed by John Hancock, who provided
the unquestioned respectability for which Samuel Adams principally
valued him—that and his inherited fortune, reputed to be the largest
in New England, which Adams regarded as the unofficial treasury of
his campaign for colonial independence.

[Hancock, then thirty-seven, was even better-looking than Dr. Warren,
and far more elegant in dress, but his personality was considerably
less engaging. When he exerted his charm, it was a conscious effort
to achieve his chief ambition in life—popular acclaim. When this effort
was not demanded of him, he relapsed into his normal nervous, ir-
ritable hypochondria. He was lavish with his money, when it seemed
likely to earn him wide applause, and even convinced some people
that he had a sincere desire to do noble things, but his political con-

Mercy Warren, intimate friend of Abigail and John Adams, wife of James Warren, was a dramatist, historian, and, as Copley revealed her, a bewitching woman.

victions at this stage in his life were wobbly. Sam Adams, for all his appreciation of Hancock's deep pockets and respectable facade, didn't wholly trust him. He was by no means alone in this attitude. John Adams deplored Hancock's incautious tongue. "Such a leaky vessel is this worthy gentleman!" he once commented.

Mercy Warren, popular blank-verse dramatist of her day and the pert, clever wife of James Warren of Plymouth, a true patriot and intimate friend of both Sam and John Adams, knew Hancock well. In her history of the American Revolution, the only one ever written by a woman, she rather acidly summed him up as follows: "This gentleman, though professedly in opposition to the Court, had oscillated between the parties until neither of them at that time had much confidence in his exertions."]

Just before the morning session of the November 5th town meeting broke up, some of Ben Faneuil's friends asked him how he thought the tea consignees would reply to the meeting's request for their resignations. He said he doubted that their response would please the voters.

"Then you'd better leave town tonight," one of his companions remarked.

"I have not yet slept out of my own house," Faneuil stoutly replied, "nor do I propose to do it till I find it absolutely necessary."

[It was, however, Guy Fawkes' Day, or Pope's Day, as it had become known in New England. (This annual occasion for folk rites commemorated the discovery and frustration of a plot by a small group of Catholics to blow up both houses of Parliament and King James I along with them on November 5, 1605, in protest against laws penalizing their religion.) Beginning as a strongly anti-Catholic ceremonial, the holiday had lost much of its religious bias by 1773. In Boston, Pope's Day had become an annual occasion for rough pranks, bizarre torchlight parades, and frequent, nondenominational street brawls. The parades often ended in bruising battles between waterfront gangs from the North End and South End of the town—practice sessions for Mackintosh's "chickens."

On Pope's Day, 1773, it seemed quite possible to Faneuil's friends that the gangs might join forces to attack the tea consignees' properties, if not their persons, although nothing was likely to happen until after dark.]

On that Friday afternoon at one o'clock, while the town meeting stood adjourned until three, Hancock and his committee called on the Clarkes and Faneuil at Richard Clarke's residence. Winslow had left for his home in Marshfield, and remained there throughout the developing crisis. The Hutchinson brothers were conferring with their father in Milton.

The blue-ribbon delegation from the town included all seven selectmen, of whom Hancock was one, and two other prominent citizens. Hancock was spokesman, but the most significant member of the Board of Selectmen was John Scollay, a stout, red-faced Scottish merchant of great common sense and cool reasonableness. In the following weeks, he worked harder than anyone else to bring about a compromise between the town and the tea consignees, even though his efforts were thoroughly undercut, in their respective ways, by Samuel Adams and Governor Hutchinson.

The committee's visit was brief and conducted with civility, but the Clarkes and Faneuil were annoyingly vague. They asked, rather insultingly, for an authenticated copy of the town's vote before they gave their answers. They also said that though Faneuil was empowered to speak for Winslow, none of them could possibly take responsibility for representing the Hutchinsons. The committee generally discredited this excuse, but Hancock, as he led his committee away, promised that the copy the consignees had asked for would be in their hands very shortly. It was, and when the town meeting reconvened at three o'clock, those present didn't have long to wait before the Clarke-Faneuil-Winslow reply arrived, addressed to the moderator. Hancock had Town Clerk William Cooper read it aloud,

> SIR:
>
> It is impossible for us to comply with the request of the Town, signified to us this day by their Com^{tee}, as we know not on what terms the tea, if any of it should be sent to our care, will come out, nor what obligations, either of a moral or pecuniary nature, we may be under to fulfil the trust that may be devolved on us. When we are acquainted with these circumstances, we shall be better qualified to give a definite answer to the request of the Town.

This was meant to be misleading, and was an obvious attempt to play for time. While it was a fact that the consignees had not received direct instructions from the East India Company as yet, they had heard from Jonathan Clarke, Palmer, and Watson. They knew of their appointments and the terms of their contracts. Even though the people at the town meeting couldn't be sure of this, they thought it altogether likely. They greeted the reading of this communiqué with hoots, and shouted for a vote. When the vote was taken, it declared unanimously that the tea consignees' response was not only unsatisfactory but "daringly affrontive" to the town.

The meeting then chose a second committee, headed by Hancock and including Sam Adams, to proceed promptly to Milton and request a reply from the Governor's sons. Their answer was to be delivered to the townspeople by the following morning. The meeting was therefore adjourned until 11 A.M., Saturday.

Next morning, as many men crowded into Faneuil Hall as had gathered there on Friday.

Hancock reported at once that his committee had found only Thomas Hutchinson, Jr., at Milton. Elisha, who had failed to show up at the Clarkes' warehouse on the day of the attack, was still missing, his absence unexplained. He may have been somewhat cowardly; he may, on the other hand, have had important business elsewhere. Tom Hutchinson's reply to the moderator of the town meeting was read aloud. It was as false and evasive as that of the other tea consignees.

> SIR:
>
> I know nothing relative to the teas referred to in the request or vote of the Town, except that one of my friends has signified to me by letter that part of it, he had reason to believe, would be consigned to me and my brother jointly. Under these circumstances, I can give no other answer to the Town at present than that if the teas should arrive, and we should be appointed factors, we shall then be sufficiently informed to answer the request of the Town. I am, for my brother and self, sir,
>
> Your humble serv^t,
> Thos. Hutchinson, Junr.

There was an angry stir in the audience, and even some impetuous cries, "To arms! To arms!" when Town Clerk Cooper finished reading. A quick, unanimous vote followed, declaring that the Hutchinsons' reply, too, was entirely unsatisfactory and daringly affrontive.

As it happened, Friday evening's Pope's Day ritual had passed without threats to the tea consignees.

John Rowe, Boston merchant, owner of the tea ship *Eleanor,* supplier to the British fleet in North American waters, and, fortunately, a dutiful diarist.

"I thought it best, however, to conceal myself for two or three hours," Faneuil confessed to Brook Watson, in a letter written Sunday. "But nothing took place more that evening than is usual on the 5th Nov.ʳ· On Friday, we received an information, which was repeated yesterday, that a number of picked men are determined to break into our house one night this week. I can hardly believe it, but these continued alarms are very disagreeable."

On Sunday, Richard Clarke, writing to Abraham Dupuis, described in detail "our present unexpected and difficult situation," and then concluded, "Besides the public transactions relative to this affair, we have repeated accounts of the continued nocturnal meetings of the leaders of the mob, and we are informed that they are determined to make the utmost efforts to prevent the sale of the teas; that their present scheme, or part of it, is to endeavor by all methods, even the most brutal, to force the consignees to give up their trust, and if they should fail in this, it is by some persons publicly asserted that the tea shall not be landed, or if it should be, that it shall be burnt."

The week that followed was deceptively quiet.

[John Rowe, who loved rural pleasures and had a countryman's sensitive awareness of seasonal changes, found nothing at all to write about in his diary until Thursday, November 11th. On that day, he noted that the wild geese, which then traveled in immense flocks, had flown southward over Boston the day before on their perennial winter migration.]

III

Governor Hutchinson, thoroughly frustrated by his disobliging Council, broke the calm on November 12th. He issued an order to John Hancock, in his capacity as colonel of the Governor's Company of Cadets, to alert his militiamen to be ready to assemble, fully armed, upon sudden call. The purpose, Hutchinson explained, was to provide strong backing for the civil magistrates "whensoever there may be a tumultuous assembly of the people, in violation of the laws."

This immediately increased tension and heightened resentment in Boston, for the signs of potential military repression of anti-administration activities were already plentiful. British soldiers—the 64th Regi-

ment of Foot, under Lieutenant-Colonel Alexander Leslie—were bar-
racked at Castle William, a venerable fort some two miles or so down
the harbor, and the men made an almost daily practice of marching
through neighboring towns in battle dress and full equipment. In addition, Admiral John Montagu, commander-in-chief of British naval
forces in American waters, had anchored his flagship *Captain*, a sixty-
four-gun ship of the line, off the Castle. *Captain* was escorted by two
frigates, *Active* and *Kingfisher*.

Hutchinson's order to Hancock brought a prompt outcry from the
Gazette, in a long editorial marked with the unmistakable sound of
Samuel Adams, that paper's most assiduous contributor. The author
of the unsigned commentary declared,

> It is very much questioned whether M. Hancock will think
> himself obliged, or even authorized by any law of this Province,
> to pay the least regard to so extraordinary a Mandate. . . .
>
> Surely the least degree of tenderness towards the people, and
> regard for their lives, would have caus'd a delay of such a Call
> till the very last extremity, unless the design is to set up a military
> tyranny. . . . What shall we say when a *native* of a country shall
> upon the slightest occasion call for the sword! How much more
> tenderness would His Excellency have shown to the people if he
> had advised his two sons and his other friends, who have it in
> their power, to prevent so fatal a necessity.

Colonel Hancock was heard to swear that he would resign his commission rather than obey the Governor's order, but he did nothing
about it officially for many weeks afterward.

On that same day, Monday, November 15th, Governor Hutchinson
wrote to Lord Dartmouth, acknowledging a letter from him that had
only just arrived, though written on August 17th. In his reply, Hutchinson gave a candid and accurate account of the situation he faced,
making it clear that he was thoroughly acquainted with the views of
those who opposed the British policies that he was obliged to try to
carry out.

> At present the spirits of the people of the town of Boston are in
> a great ferment. Every thing that has been in my power, without
> the Council, I have done and continue to do for the preservation
> of the peace and good order of the town. If I had the aid which
> I think the Council might give, my endeavors would be more

effectual. They profess to disapprove of the tumultuous, violent proceedings of the people, but they wish to see the professed ends of the people in such proceedings attained in a regular way. And, instead of joining with me in proper measures to discourage an opposition to the landing of the teas expected, one and another of the gentlemen of the greatest influence intimate that the best thing that can be done to quiet the people would be the refusal of the gentlemen to whom the teas are consigned to execute the trust; and they declare they would do it if it was their case, and would advise all their connections to do it. Nor will they ever countenance a measure which shall tend to carry into execution an act of Parliament which lays taxes upon the colonies for the purpose of a revenue.

The merchants, who, though in general they declare against mobs and violence, yet they as generally wish the teas may not be imported.

The persons to whom the teas are consigned declare that, whilst they can be protected from violence to their persons, they will not give way to the unreasonable demands which have been made of them.

IV

That essential physical protection seemed altogether lacking two evenings later.

Early on Wednesday, November 17th, Hancock's ship *Hayley*, bringing Jonathan Clarke home from England, nosed through the maze of islands, rocks, and sandbars that cluttered Boston Harbor between the open sea and the town's waterfront, and tied up at its owner's wharf.

All of the Clarke family, and a few close friends, quickly gathered at Richard Clarke's residence when they heard that Jonathan had returned. When the fervor of the affectionate reunion that followed had abated enough to allow Jonathan a few moments by himself, he wrote a hasty note to Edward Wheler, chairman of the East India Company.

"After a long detention in the English Channel, and a pretty long passage, I arrived here this morning from England," he began, "and there being a vessel to sail for London within a few hours, gives me an opportunity of writing you a few lines on the subject of the consignment of tea made to our house by the Hon'ble East India Company, in which I had your friendly assistance, and of which I shall always retain a grateful sense.

"I find that this measure is an unpopular one," Jonathan continued, in a notable understatement, "and before my arrival some measures have been taken to oblige my friends to make a resignation of the trust, which they have not thought fit to comply with. They have wrote to our friend Mr. Abraham Dupuis very particularly respecting the measures that have been adopted, and to that account I must beg leave to refer you, as I have not time to repeat it by this opportunity, but I shall keep the Company fully advised in future.

"I fully see that we shall meet with difficulty in executing this trust," Jonathan acknowledged, "but our utmost endeavors shall be exerted to fulfill the orders we may receive from the Company." (This note did not reach Chairman Wheler until January 5, 1774, by which time the issue had been settled forever, in its memorable way.)

That evening, there was a large, merry dinner party at Richard Clarke's house, but it came to an abrupt, terrifying end.

At the party's height, a sudden bray of horns and piercing squeal of whistles from outside silenced the happy chatter of the diners. Whistles and horns were familiar signals for rallying street gangs in the Boston of those troubled days, and a large, noisy crowd had congregated in School Street.

A neighbor of Clarke's, subsequently identified in the *Gazette* only as "a worthy gentleman sustaining an important public office in the town," came out of his house and tried to talk the crowd into dispersing.

"There'll undoubtedly be a town meeting tomorrow," he told them, "where I hope all will be settled to your general satisfaction."

The crowd seemed inclined to quiet down and go home, but at this delicate moment a log of firewood came flying through the air and struck a man standing near the would-be peacemaker. The crowd assumed that the missile had come from inside the Clarke residence, and its mood instantly changed.

There came a furious pounding on the Clarke front door.

The women of the party were hurriedly escorted upstairs, which seemed to promise greater security, but with them dashed a reckless young man—some said it was Isaac Clarke—who ran to a bedroom window overlooking the crowded yard. He flung open the window and shouted, "You rascals! Be gone, or I'll blow your brains out!" He foolishly followed up this command by firing a pistol into the crowd. He had not taken aim, and hit no one, but the crowd understandably reacted with explosive anger.

It "violently attacked the house . . . & with Stones Brickbats Clubs & Cord wood Sticks continued for the space of two hours breaking the windows & window Shutters & doing other damage whereby the Lives of the family were in imminent danger notwithstanding many efforts to disperse the People." So did the Clarkes breathlessly describe their ordeal in a petition that they and the other tea consignees composed the following day for the Governor and Council.

Anne Hulton, sister of the British customs man who called Dr. Warren a rascally apothecary, wrote to England that "a great number of stones each so large as to have killed any person they had hit were thrown about the table where the family were at supper, but Providence directed 'em so that they did not fall on any person. All the avenues to the house . . . were guarded . . . to prevent Mr. Clarke escaping. This was beyond anything of the kind since we came here."

V

Word of Jonathan Clarke's rowdy reception flew around Boston.

The next morning, William Cooper, the town clerk, issued a hurried call to the voters to assemble at a special town meeting that same day. The meeting, correctly assuming that Jonathan had brought his associates more specific information than they had had before, dispatched another committee to request the immediate resignation of the tea consignees.

This time, the committee returned with an answer indicating that the town's efforts at negotiation were hopeless. "In answer to the message we have this day [November 18th] received from the town," the consignees wrote, "we beg leave to say that we have not yet received any order from the East India Company respecting the expected teas, but we are now further acquainted that our friends in England have entered into general engagements in our behalf, merely of a commercial nature, which puts it out of our power to comply with the request of the town."

James Otis was a brilliant lawyer and leading spokesman for the colonies when Copley painted this portrait. By 1773 his keen mind was in sad disarray.

After Cooper's public reading of this cold reply, the moderator, without allowing for discussion or voting, abruptly adjourned the meeting.

"This sudden dissolution struck more terror into the consignees than the most minatory resolves," wrote Governor Hutchinson.

Richard Clarke's haughty defiance of the "mob-ility" was by now fast fading. Anne Hulton reported that he had lately been heard to swear "he will be tore to pieces before he will desert the trust reposed on him by the Consigners." But, after experiencing mob violence both at his warehouse and at his home, Clarke, whose health was not robust, was looking rather anxiously for an escape route.

At this juncture, on November 18th some of his closest friends urged him and his associates to shift the prickly burden of their predicament to the Governor and his Council. In consequence, the tea consignees sent a formal petition to those gentlemen that evening, begging "leave to resign themselves, and the property committed to their care, to your Excellency and Honors, as the guardians and protectors of the people, humbly praying that measures may be directed for the landing and securing of the teas until your petitioners can be at liberty, openly and safely, to dispose of the same, or until they can receive directions from their constituents."

Governor Hutchinson later wrote that although he was accused of having instigated this particular maneuver, he knew nothing about it until the next morning, Friday, November 19th, when he rode into town from Milton in his elegant carriage to preside at a regular Council meeting. When he did become aware of it, he said, he felt certain it wouldn't succeed.

Only eight of the twenty-eight members of the Council, which was elected by the House of Representatives, met with Hutchinson that day. Two of them, Isaac Royal of Medford and William Brattle of Cambridge, were eminent Tories. James Bowdoin, a leading Whig, and James Otis, the patriots' "flame of Fire" of John Adams's admiring younger days, now sadly guttering, were the principal anti-administration figures, though they were backed by at least two-thirds of the Council.

[Otis had become a most uncertain quantity. His failing mind had worried his intimates for several years. He had had to be taken away in a straitjacket in 1771, but had recovered sufficiently by this time to be free of restraint and back in his former haunts. His mind fluc-

tuated, though, between lucidity and wild imaginings, his orator's voice
sometimes ringing with its old, thrilling challenge to British oppression, sometimes reduced to incoherence or embarrassingly abject apologies to Governor Hutchinson for having ever opposed him.]

"The Governor laid before the Council the distracted state of the
Province," Hutchinson later wrote of this meeting in his *History*. He
declared that the inhabitants of Boston were in possession of the
process of government, that he had done his best to preserve peace
and to suppress "all riotous assemblies of the people," but without
success. A mob had attacked Richard Clarke's house, he said, and the
tea consignees feared further violence when the tea ships arrived. They
were expected any hour. The Governor asked for the Council's advice
and help.

He had roused little sympathy.

"This riot was not of the most enormous kind," drily remarked one
of the Council members, not identified. Mobs were frequent in England in Sir Robert Walpole's time, he recalled. And why? Because
the people would not stand for the Cider Act. By rioting, they had
forced Parliament to rescind it. If the people of Boston behaved simi-
larly now, it was because they had plenty of provocation; they resented
this latest unconstitutional act of Parliament.

Another Council member spoke up, in similar vein. He dreaded the
consequences of the Tea Act, he said, and in his opinion the only way
to prevent them was for the consignees to resign their trust.

At this point, Thomas Flucker, Secretary of the Province, brought
in the petition from the Clarkes and their associates. There was lively
debate over its contents. The Council member who had previously
called for their resignations made haste to say that of course he hadn't
meant that they were to resign their trust to the Governor and Council. *We* shouldn't accept custody of the tea, he protested to his fellow-
members, lest we become financially liable for any damage that might
befall it.

A wrangle developed, and the Governor was urged to adjourn the
meeting until the following Tuesday, November 23rd.

On that day, Richard Clarke, signing himself "your affectionate
Father and faithful Friend," wrote a brief note to his sons, bowing out
of the conflict. He said simply that he would be "out of Town for a
few days." He empowered Jonathan and Isaac to make whatever agree-

ment they thought suitable in regard to the tea, and said he would fully support their eventual decision when asked to do so.

Clarke didn't mention where he was going, but he, like all the other tea consignees, had a summer home outside Boston, and presumably retreated there. Governor Hutchinson wrote to a friend that "old Mr. Clarke" (no older than the Governor himself), "his constitution being hurt by the repeated attacks made upon him," had "retired into the country."

When the Governor came into Boston to meet with his Council on November 23rd, so few of them showed up that he was obliged once more to adjourn the meeting, this time until Saturday, November 27th.

On the 27th, nine Council members convened with Hutchinson. They included the aged Samuel Danforth, Judge of the Court of Common Pleas and adviser to successive royal governors of Massachusetts Bay for the previous thirty-four years. Danforth, a quiet man known to have royalist leanings, had graduated from Harvard in 1715.

James Bowdoin was the most dynamic presence. He spoke up at once, saying that he had put his thoughts in writing, and begged the Governor's leave to read them aloud and table the paper.

Hutchinson balked at this. He knew altogether too well that Bowdoin's thoughts would be diametrically opposed to his own and to the policy he felt duty-bound to uphold. The procedure would be irregular, he said. It would "make an ill precedent."

Arguments rumbled on for some time. It was obvious to all that the predominant sentiment of the Council matched that of the town meeting. Furthermore, the Governor suspected that Bowdoin's "thoughts" were intended more for the public than for the Council records. Still, to make any progress at all, he was finally obliged to let them be read aloud.

As he had feared, they were inflammatory. The text was devoted largely to "a few observations" on the "very unhappy" situation between Great Britain and the colonies, which, over the course of several years, had finally led to the events that had provoked the present petition from the consignees for protection and relief. Bowdoin's paper expressed once more, with clarity and dignity, a firm denial of Parliament's right to tax the colonies, declaring that to submit to it would reduce the colonists to a condition "little better than slavery." If, he argued, the Council were now to enact measures for landing and securing the tea, as the consignees requested, it would simply be allying it-

self with Parliament's aims, for once the tea was landed, it immediately
became subject to duty. For the Council to act in that manner would
also be for it to contradict the resolutions of both Council and House
of Representatives during the last session of the Massachusetts General
Court, early in 1773. Those resolutions had expressed essentially what
Bowdoin had said earlier on the subject of taxation. To act counter to
them, he pointed out, would be "altogether inexpedient and im-
proper."

[Hutchinson well remembered his strenuous opposition to those resolutions of the General Court and how greatly that action had increased
his unpopularity. He also recalled the startled reactions of Lord Dartmouth, so generally inclined to a tolerant and sympathetic attitude
toward the colonies. Dartmouth had written that those resolutions
were "replete with doctrines of the most dangerous nature, the latter
of which does in direct terms question the authority of Parliament to
make laws binding upon the subjects of that province in any case whatsoever." There was no time, he added, to report wider and more ma-
ture consideration of the action of the Massachusetts General Court,
for a packet was about to sail. Dartmouth concluded, in haste, that "all
that I have at present in comment from the King is to recommend you
to avoid further discussion whatsoever upon these questions."]

Well, Hutchinson could scarcely avoid discussing them now.
After Bowdoin had finished with the salient issues, he rather sum-
marily dismissed the plea of the tea consignees for protection. Let them
call one of the justices of the peace, "they being invested by law with
all the authority necessary for the protection of His Majesty's subjects."
The Council, he said, hadn't heard of any such call by the petitioners.
(Yet the Council could hardly have failed to know that Justice Hatch
was present at the warehouse fracas, and was powerless to stop it, and
that at Richard Clarke's residence the attack had been so sudden, there
had been no opportunity to call a justice of the peace.)
The Council couldn't assume responsibility for the tea, Bowdoin
continued, without making itself financially liable in case of damages.
All it could say, finally, was that "as they have seen, with regret, some
late disturbances, and have advised . . . prosecuting the authors of
them, so they will in all legal methods endeavor to the utmost of their
power to prevent them in future."

Hutchinson was disgusted and angry. He at once warned the Council of the probable consequences if these expressed sentiments reached England. They would be highly resented there, he promised, and would undoubtedly be used as an excuse for changing the constitution of the province. This warning caused enough uneasiness and doubt among the Council members to cause them to request a further postponement of decision. All right, said Hutchinson, they might have until Monday, November 29th.

VI

On Saturday, meanwhile, much more pragmatic discussions had been in progress between Jonathan and Isaac Clarke, on the one hand, and the full roster of Boston's Board of Selectmen, on the other. Earlier in the day, Jonathan had called on John Scollay, the sensible, deeply concerned chairman of the Board, and requested that he and his brother be allowed to meet with the selectmen at their earliest convenience. This overture seemed auspicious, so Scollay had set four o'clock the same afternoon as the time of their appointment.

The Clarkes arrived to find the full Board in attendance. Jonathan opened the discussion with a bald lie. He declared that he was very unhappy at having incurred the displeasure of his fellow-citizens, but he hadn't sought the East India Company's appointment, he said; he was "wholly passive in the affair." It doubtless seemed to him more prudent to lie about it, now that he had sampled the fierce public temper, than to tell the truth. Yet, even as Scollay repeated this unexpected statement, in a subsequent letter to Arthur Lee, in London, he made a parenthetical comment: "(this by some is said to be not true)."

Under the circumstances, Jonathan Clarke continued, he felt that "it was unreasonable that he and the others should suffer."

Keeping our private feelings out of this, Scollay replied, in effect, we gather that the people won't be satisfied with anything less than your sending the tea back where it came from.

That's impossible, Clarke replied. It would be contrary to the Acts of Trade. The tea and the vessel would both be confiscated. Thus, the consignees would become directly responsible for the Company's loss. They might well bring ruin upon themselves.

Not necessarily, some of the selectmen suggested. A way might be found around the difficulty. The consignees could declare to the East India Company that when they found that the tea could not be landed without the utmost hazard, they had decided to return it to the Company rather than risk its total loss. They could send along a formal statement of protest against those who had obstructed them in their attempt to carry out the Company's plans. In this way, the selectmen suggested, they would probably be warmly thanked for saving the Company's property. On the other hand, if they persisted in trying to land the tea, they might well earn the Company's resentment, "and very justly," for not having preserved the cargo when they had it in their power to do so.

"We had a long conversation with this gentleman and his brother on the subject," Scollay wrote, and one wonders how well tempers were kept. The selectmen could not have had much patience left. "We" had already "labored night and day in the affair," Scollay assured Arthur Lee, and yet "all our efforts could not produce an agreement between them and the Town. The town's people thought they had been ill-treated by them at the late town meetings; therefore they were now on their part determined that the teas should not be landed; so the consignees were on their part obstinate, and would be noways active in sending it back."

Scollay felt certain the situation could have been saved (and the Boston Tea Party prevented). If only the consignees, when the town first asked them to resign, had offered to store the tea, allowing a committee from the town to inspect it at will, and to pay no duty on it until they could obtain the East India Company's decision in the matter (which, Scollay felt, could hardly have been other than a decision to have the tea returned), the outcome would have been very different. He was confident that the commissioners of the customs "would have consented to this arrangement, the Town would have accepted the offer, and every thing would have been preserved from destruction."

Instead, when the Clarkes' conference with the selectmen on Saturday afternoon, November 27th, had at last come to its tired end, it had little to show for its efforts. Jonathan Clarke would assure them only that nothing underhanded would be attempted. The first tea ship to arrive—and it would undoubtedly be the *Dartmouth*, expected hourly —would come up to town, he said. Then, as soon as he had had a chance to read the London mail that Captain Hall would be bringing

him, he and the other tea consignees would send their latest proposals
to the selectmen.

VII

But, by the next day, there was an abrupt change in the situation. The
time for academic discussion had at last run out.

At ten o'clock on Saturday evening, after a day of fresh breezes, hazy
weather, and scattered rain, the *Dartmouth* sailed to within two miles
of Boston Light, dropped anchor, and sent a boat ashore for a pilot.

At four o'clock on Sunday morning, the pilot came aboard, and by
six, with a favoring tide and the wind at West North West, the first of
the tea ships began its slow progress up the narrow channel that wound
among the geological hazards of the harbor.

At eleven in the morning, the tide beginning to ebb, *Dartmouth* was
maneuvered into position astern of the Admiral's flagship, off Castle
William, and again dropped anchor.

By then, alert harbor-watchers had brought word of the ship's arrival
to Boston's Committee of Correspondence, headed by Samuel Adams.
A courier from town, briefed in advance, had also galloped off to Milton to notify the Governor. Both Adams and Hutchinson moved at
once, in their opposing ways, to deal with the situation. Adams was
determined to trap the tea consignees in a predicament from which
they, and especially the Governor, could not escape. Hutchinson was
equally determined to prevent the trap from opening.

Their respective tactics were based on their thorough knowledge of
the fact that if the tea were brought to dock, it would be subject to
duty; could not be unloaded without paying duty; could not be sent
back to England without the approval of the customs officers, who
could not legally grant that approval until the duty had been paid;
and, in any event, could not leave the harbor without a pass from the
Governor, who would certainly not grant it, in direct violation of his
oath to uphold the Acts of Trade, unless the duty had been paid.

Furthermore, the trade regulations in force throughout the Empire
required that duty imposed on any cargo must be paid within twenty
days of its arrival in port. If the duty remained unpaid after the ex-
piration of that time, the cargo was subject to immediate confiscation.
The twenty-day limit on *Dartmouth*'s cargo would expire at midnight

on December 16th. If its cargo were to be confiscated by the customs men, Adams and his friends were confident that it would sooner or later be sold to the tea-hungry public, a result they were relentlessly determined to prevent.

All of these snares could be avoided if the tea ship were to anchor below Castle William, regarded, for customs purposes, as the outer limit of the harbor. At that anchorage, the ship's cargo was not subject to duty. From there, if necessary, it could be returned to England with minimal complications.

In view of these considerations, Samuel Adams sent orders from the Boston Committee of Correspondence to Captain Hall, of the *Dartmouth*, to bring his ship up to town at the earliest opportunity or risk the "utmost peril" to his reputation and his person. At the same time, Governor Hutchinson dispatched orders to Captain Hall by the shore pilot—or so he later stated—to keep his ship off Castle William until he received further instructions from Hutchinson.

This, at any rate, was the situation as Governor Hutchinson described it in his *History*, completed after he had gone into exile in England in 1775. Since Hutchinson was ordinarily a truthful man, with a respected historian's sense of responsibility for keeping the record straight, it seems reasonable to accept his word that he tried to prevent the tea ships from sailing into the jurisdiction of the customs men. He wrote that both the tea consignees and Francis Rotch, owner of the *Dartmouth*, had consented to that course of action. Yet no independent contemporary evidence has been found to support Hutchinson's word.

There is, however, the indisputable evidence of *Dartmouth*'s log that the pilot came aboard at 4 A.M. on Sunday, November 28th, and that at 11 A.M. the vessel anchored behind the Admiral's flagship, off Castle William. This would seem to indicate that Captain Hall was obeying orders brought to him by the pilot. True, the tide was beginning to ebb, but that fact alone would not have prevented the vessel from sailing on to dock in town.

Meanwhile, the Committee of Correspondence and the Loyal Nine went into frenetic production of printed alarms and written calls for support. The Loyal Nine prepared, and Benjamin Edes printed, handbills for the trees and street corners, the text to be copied in as many of Monday's newspapers as found it fit to print. The proclamation read:

FRIENDS!   BRETHREN!   COUNTRYMEN!

That worst of plagues, the detested tea, shipped for this port by
the East India Company, is now arrived in this harbor; the hour
of destruction or manly oppositions to the machinations of tyranny
stares you in the face; every friend to his country, to himself, and
posterity is now called upon to meet at Faneuil Hall at nine
o'clock this day [Monday] (at which time the bells will ring), to
make a united and successful resistance to this last, worst and most
destructive measure of administration.

Boston, November 29, 1773.

Dr. Joseph Warren and Dr. Benjamin Church, that busy informer,
were at the same time drafting an urgent invitation to the Committees
of Correspondence of Cambridge, Charlestown, Dorchester, and Roxbury, on the immediate fringe of Boston, to come to Monday's meeting
at Faneuil Hall and bring as many of their fellowtownsmen as possible.

"Gentlemen," the single text ran, "a part of the tea shipped by the
East India Company is now arrived in this harbor, and we look upon
ourselves bound to give you the earliest intimation of it, and we desire
that you would favor us with your company at Faneuil Hall, at 9
o'clock this forenoon, there to give us your advice what steps are to be
immediately taken in order effectually to prevent the impending evil;
and we request you to urge your friends in the town to which you be-
long to be in readiness to exert themselves in the most resolute manner
to assist this town in their efforts for saving this oppressed country. [At
this point, Dr. Warren's handwriting left off, and Dr. Church's began.]
Should the business of the town prevent your punctual compliance
with our request at the hour mentioned, let us entreat you to send as
many friends to our assistance at this important crisis as you can possibly spare, and to favor us with your personal attendance at the very
moment after effecting the business of the day."

This plea was postdated November 29th, and copies were dispatched
as soon as possible by mounted messengers. Paul Revere was undoubtedly one of them, since this was a regular chore of his. The
Boston Committee of Correspondence wanted its invitations delivered
in ample time to alert those other communities to its call for support
before dawn on Monday.

At noon on Sunday, the Board of Selectmen, somewhat awed by

Paul Revere, at his workbench as Copley painted him, was a courier of the Boston Committee of Correspondence and is thought to have taken part in the Tea Party.

their apparent disrespect for the Lord and possible infringement of the
Blue Laws, convened at Faneuil Hall to await the Clarkes' promised
proposals. When they grew tired of waiting, they sent a courier to
Jonathan's residence. Nobody was at home. The selectmen then adjourned until five o'clock. When they met again, only to find that
there was still no word from the tea consignees, they sent messengers
to the Boston homes of both Clarke brothers, the Governor's sons, and
Faneuil.

[Josiah Winslow was still ailing (he died about a year later), at his
home in Marshfield. After his one frightening experience with the
others at Clarkes' warehouse, Winslow retreated to Marshfield, and
thereafter let his partner, Faneuil, make all the necessary decisions for
them both.]

The selectmen stayed in session until nine o'clock that evening, hop-
ing vainly that replies from the tea consignees would arrive in time to
permit them to issue a call for a legal town meeting Monday morning.
This would automatically take precedence over the rump caucus con-
voked by the Committee of Correspondence, and give the proceedings
the weight of legitimacy.

Long before the selectmen gave up, one of them, "finding the storm
arising," as Scollay put it, had privately sent an urgent note to one of
Jonathan Clarke's brothers-in-law. (Though not identified in the old
accounts, this was almost certainly John Singleton Copley, as later
developments will indicate.) The note told that gentleman that if he
cared anything for Jonathan and the others, he would make the most
strenuous effort to locate him and persuade him and his associates to
respond to the selectmen at once. The answer came back promptly that
Jonathan's brother-in-law had no idea where Jonathan was, but he'd
do his best to find him and persuade him to respond "early next morning."

An hour later, far down the harbor, two customs officers came aboard
the *Dartmouth* from Castle William—"we being the first ship ever
boarded in this manner," wrote Mate Alexander Hodgdon indignantly
in the ship's journal. "Which happened on account of our having the
East India Company's *accursed dutiable* tea on board." The underscoring was his. Hodgdon, a future treasurer of the State of Massachusetts,
was a Whig, and dared to put in the log a sentiment that might well

Province House, where Governor Hutchinson regularly met with his recalcitrant Council, stood on the opposite side of Marlborough Street from
Old South Church.

earn him the displeasure of Captain Hall, who favored the royalist side.

By their unprecedented action of boarding the *Dartmouth* off Castle William, the customs men had made it impossible thereafter for Governor Hutchinson, with his stern sense of duty and honor, to do other than insist upon strict adherence to the Acts of Trade, even when his avowed intention had been to dodge that necessity. Why the customs men should deliberately have frustrated the Governor's plan for the tea ships remains a tantalizing mystery, and appears to have no explanation more reasonable than that it was a thoroughgoing bureaucratic mixup. By doing so, they played directly into Samuel Adams's hands, which they never conceivably would have done on purpose.

VIII

Monday dawned fair, and *Dartmouth's* captain went up to town, having concluded that he had better consult with his ship's owners before weighing anchor and proceeding to a town dock.

The selectmen had not yet heard a word from the tea consignees, and by now it was too late.

By nine o'clock, Faneuil Hall was found to be far too small to accommodate the huge crowd that was assembling. The leaders decided to move to "Dr. Sewall's meeting house," better known as Old South Church, which stood on the northeast corner of Marlborough and Milk Streets. This was the largest auditorium in Boston, spacious enough to hold most of the "five or six thousand of respectable inhabitants," as Scollay described them, "men of the best character and of the first fortune," who had come to confer that day. The size of the crowd becomes all the more significant when one realizes that it was the equivalent of one-third of Boston's entire population at that time.

Governor Hutchinson, meeting gloomily at about the same hour with his Council in Province House, almost directly across Marlborough Street from Old South Church, thought less highly of the great gathering, but even he had to admit that it wasn't a mob.

"Although it consisted principally of the lower ranks of the people," Hutchinson commented, "and even journeymen tradesmen were brought to increase the number, and the rabble were not excluded, yet there were divers gentlemen of good fortune among them."

Hutchinson was about to reach the end of his wholly unsatisfactory

Old South Church, or Meeting House, as it appeared about 1800. One group of Tea Party "Indians" ran from there to Griffin's Wharf down Milk Street, seen here.

sessions with the Council. At its meeting on this final day, Bowdoin read again the text of his "thoughts," which had so antagonized the Governor on the previous Saturday. The phraseology had not been altered appreciably, despite Hutchinson's warnings. When Bowdoin finished reading, the Governor cried out, "But will you gentlemen give me no advice as to how I should deal with these disorders now prevailing?" Bowdoin replied stiffly that the advice given in his paper was intended for that purpose.

This was "worse than nothing," Hutchinson complained in a letter to his frequent confidant Governor William Tryon of New York. "They drew up a declaration of grievances which cause this disordered state of the people, declare against doing anything for the protection of the tea because the duty on it is unconstitutional, and conclude with desiring me to direct the justices, etc., to keep the peace. An indiscreet countenancing and encouraging [of] the disorders!"

As for the rebellious citizens gathered across the street in Old South Church, Hutchinson later wrote, "The people continued together in possession of all the powers of government, for any purpose they thought fit."

"What am I in duty bound to do?" he lamented, with underscoring, to Lieutenant-Governor Oliver, urging the latter to bring Secretary Flucker along with him to Milton for dinner, in order that he might have the benefit of their collective advice in his increasingly isolated position.

Jonathan Williams was elected moderator of the immense mass meeting that convened at Old South Church on that Monday morning, November 29th—a meeting containing delegates from at least five other communities and which was obliged to extend its sessions through Tuesday.

"Nothing can be more inflammatory than the speeches and declarations made on this occasion," Hutchinson declared to his friend Tryon. "They soon resolved that the tea should not be landed, that no duty should be paid, and that it should be sent back to England."

Selectman Scollay thought the proceedings were very well behaved. "I will only say," he reported to Arthur Lee, "that it is the observation of persons unprejudiced, and of character, who attended these meetings, which consisted of all sorts, *Whig and Tory,* that the utmost decorum was observed.

A silhouette portrait of Francis Rotch, owner of the tea ship *Dartmouth*. It was done years after the Tea Party, but clearly caught his independent spirit.

"Through the whole of their debates," he continued, "although they were determined the tea should not be landed subject to a duty, yet it was apparent that their only view in sending it back was not only to render the scheme of Administration abortive but to preserve the tea from destruction. This ran through the whole of their reasoning on the subject. To accomplish this, every step that could be taken (consistent with their intentions of its going back) was taken to preserve it."

The tea consignees, meanwhile, had fled to the protection of "amiable & good" Colonel Leslie, as Miss Hulton described him, at Castle William.

When the consignees were told of the resolves of Monday morning's meeting, and heard that they had been given until three o'clock that afternoon to agree to them, "they determined to remove to the Castle," Hutchinson reported, "having obtained an order from me for their reception." They left town at about the time the mass meeting reconvened.

"They apprehended they should be seized, and may be, tarred and feathered and carted—an American torture—in order to compel them to a compliance," wrote Governor Hutchinson to Lord Dartmouth. This seems to have been an entirely unwarranted fear, though understandable enough in the minds of men who had already experienced the riotous attacks on the Clarke warehouse and residence.

In a subsequent letter to Lord Dartmouth, he wrote, in regard to the resolutions of the November 29–30 mass meetings in Boston, "I can scarcely think they will prosecute these mad resolves; yet it is possible, and if it becomes probable I shall be under the necessity of withdrawing to the Castle also, in order to defeat them as far as shall be in my power."

The Governor was probably relieved to see the consignees take refuge in the Castle. As he had written to Governor Tryon, Richard Clarke's friends had brought heavy pressure on his sons and the other consignees to give in and agree to the town's terms. Hutchinson was afraid that they might weaken. "I hope they will not comply with such monstrous demands," he confided in a note to his youngest son, Billy.

There was little likelihood of that. As the town's anger grew, so did the consignees' stubbornness.

When the crowd at Old South Church reassembled, and found that no reply had yet come from the tea consignees, its members angrily decided to waste no more time. They voted unanimously that the tea in the *Dartmouth* must be returned to England in that same vessel, and at the earliest possible moment.

Young Francis Rotch, twenty-three, rose to protest. He and his brothers owned the ship. He said he was obliged to put his protest on record, for the Rotches simply could not comply with the town's wishes without risking seizure of their vessel, and incurring financial ruin.

The meeting overrode his protest, voting without dissent that Rotch be directed not to enter the cargo of tea at the customhouse, at his peril. Captain Hall, who was also present, was warned not to permit any of the tea to be landed, at *his* peril, but he was told to bring his ship up to town from below the Castle at once and anchor it. Hall left the meeting to comply.

A motion was then made, and unanimously passed, that in order to make certain that these orders were obeyed, a guard of twenty-five men be assigned to the ship every night that it lay in port, beginning immediately. Captain Edward Proctor was appointed to command the first night's guard. Volunteers to fill that roster were asked to leave their names with the moderator; Paul Revere and three members of the Loyal Nine were among them. (The guard went aboard *Dartmouth* that night at 9 P.M., even though the ship was still anchored astern of the Admiral's flagship.) Volunteers for successive nights' duty could offer their services henceforth at Edes & Gill's printing office. (Rosters [see Appendix] were filled mostly from the ranks of the Governor's Company of Cadets, who reported for duty fully armed, despite the Governor's protest to Hancock.)

At this point, John Hancock suddenly announced that John Singleton Copley had just brought him word from the consignees. This announcement caught everyone's attention and hushed the audience. The consignees, Copley had reported, had not received their instructions from the East India Company until the evening before, from Captain Hall's ship, and then had been "so dispersed" that they were unable to confer in time to send their promised reply to the Board of Selectmen when expected. They asked a further extension of time until the following morning.

There were groans and indignant mutterings over this. Dr. Thomas Young, one of Samuel Adams' closest friends and confidants, shouted that "the only way to get rid of the tea is to throw it overboard." The meeting finally agreed, however, that "out of great tenderness to these persons, and from a strong desire to bring this matter to a conclusion, notwithstanding the time they had hitherto expended upon them, to no purpose," the tea consignees' latest request would be granted.

Just before adjournment, the audience's startled attention was drawn to the fact that Governor Hutchinson had ordered all of Boston's justices of the peace to "meet and use their endeavors to suppress any routs or riots of the people that might happen."

"Is it not the sense of this meeting," the moderator asked tartly, "that the Governor's conduct herein carries a designed reflection upon the people here met, and is solely calculated to serve the views of Administration?"

It was indeed. The vote was a resounding "Yes." There were no dissenters.

IX

There then commenced a singular ordeal for John Singleton Copley, thirty-five years old and at the peak of his distinguished powers as an artist. Copley, a shy, timid man, abhorred politics and despised contention. He also had an unreasoning fear of being on the water. Now that he had summoned the nerve to volunteer to carry messages between the embattled consignees and the hostile town, he found himself at the very center of a furious controversy and obliged to travel to and from the Castle by small boat in order to accomplish his self-appointed mission.

Copley suffered with a rankling sense of inferiority at being a portrait painter in a society that customarily lumped portrait painters with sign painters. The fact that he was unquestionably the best limner, as people called him, in America, earned a handsome income, owned a large part of Beacon Hill, lived there in a fine house next to John Hancock's, and was a member by marriage of one of the first families of Boston helped to shore up his self-esteem. Still, he had to muster unusual courage and resolve to volunteer to act as intermediary between a large and angry group of the sort of people among whom he had been brought up on Boston's waterfront and a smaller but equally indignant and stubborn group of the local gentry, whose familiar he had since become. Copley made an ideal choice for ambassador between the opposing sides, though, for he was liked and trusted by both.

But his mission failed.

When Copley left the meeting to begin his fearsome voyage to the Castle, it was already dark, which greatly increased the distastefulness of the mission, but he was rowed to the fort through calm waters and under bright stars. Upon his arrival, he found, to his dismay, that his brothers-in-law and their colleagues, taking courage from their surroundings of cannon and friendly soldiery, had prepared a defiant reply to the selectmen, "absolutely refusing to do what they had before informed us the people expected."

Copley accepted this missive with strong misgivings, and after he was back on the cobbles of Boston, he felt overwhelmed by doubts and fears. He paced the waterfront for a few minutes in an agony of indecision, then asked his oarsman to row him back to the Castle. Copley felt certain that such a flat rejection of the town's demand as he had brought with him might have the most serious consequences to the persons and properties of his friends.

The consignees were astonished to see him back again so soon, but were sufficiently impressed by his worried pleas to agree upon a more conciliatory message—and, surprisingly, a concession. They wrote a second note to the selectmen, ignoring the existence of the ostensibly illegal town meeting:

"We still retain a disposition to do all in our power to give satisfaction to the Town," this note read, "but, as we understood . . . at Messrs. Clarke's interview with you last Saturday, that this can be effected by nothing less than our sending back the tea, we beg leave to say that this is utterly out of our power to do, but we do now declare to you our readiness to store the teas until we shall have an opportunity of writing to our constituents and shall receive their further orders respecting them, and we do most sincerely wish that the Town, considering the unexpected difficulties devolved upon us, will be satisfied with what we now offer."

Copley's apprehensions were a bit allayed by this, and he presented the letter, not to the moderator but to John Scollay, at the reconvened meeting the following morning at nine, with some hope of improving the situation.

His hope quickly proved to be groundless. The meeting took only a few minutes to dismiss the latest word from the tea consignees as entirely unsatisfactory. Before Copley could make an effort to keep negotiations alive, Sheriff Stephen Greenleaf, an amiable, aging Tory, arrived with a proclamation from Governor Hutchinson. (After the

Governor had dispatched it, early that morning, he had half-jokingly commented to his son Billy, "I may soon have to take refuge in the Castle myself.") Greenleaf asked the moderator for permission to read the proclamation, and the audience voted unanimously to let him do so.

Hutchinson, as anxious as Francis Rotch to have his position in the controversy become a matter of record, accused the meeting of "openly violating, defying and setting at naught the good and wholesome laws of the Province and the constitution of government under which they live." Accordingly, the Governor continued, "In faithfulness to my trust, and as His Majesty's representative within the Province, I am bound to bear testimony against this violation of the laws, and I warn and exhort you and require you, and each of you thus unlawfully assembled, forthwith to disperse and to surcease all further unlawful proceedings at your utmost peril."

When the Sheriff finished reading the proclamation, the audience immediately expressed its reaction in "a loud and very general hiss." When the moderator asked ironically if those present would obey the Governor's instructions, the vote was a clamorous "No," without dissent.

At this point, Copley, who wasn't yet ready to capitulate in his campaign of diplomacy, stood up, doubtless on shaking legs, and told the huge, hostile crowd that he would go back to the Castle and try to persuade the Clarkes and their associates to come before this meeting themselves. He asked to be granted two hours in which to accomplish the errand. First, though, he wanted the crowd's assurance that his relatives and friends would be treated with civility, "though they might be of different sentiments with this body," and allowed afterward to return in safety to the Castle. His questions were put to a vote, and the response this time was affirmative.

The meeting was adjourned until two o'clock, and Copley once more set out for the Castle in a rowboat. The day was gray and cold, the harbor waters choppy.

At two o'clock, Copley hadn't returned, but the meeting proceeded with arrangements to solve the tea problem to its own satisfaction. It once again summoned Francis Rotch and Captain Hall before it. Was it the firm resolution of this body, the moderator asked once again, as if to make certain there were no backsliders present, that the tea in *Dartmouth* should be returned to Britain in that same vessel? The

meeting once more declared unanimously that it was. Francis Rotch
again replied that he must formally protest against these proceedings,
but that since he had no alternative, he would comply with the resolution of the meeting. Captain Hall agreed to sail the tea back where it
came from.

John Rowe, owner of the *Eleanor*, and a man named Timmins,
agent for Captain Coffin's brig *Beaver*, were then summoned to appear
immediately at Old South Church. Rowe, thoroughly unhappy by now
that Captain Bruce had been so imprudent as to accept part of the
East India consignment for outbound cargo, and especially so since he,
Rowe, had already purchased a return cargo for the *Eleanor* which
was waiting on the wharf to be loaded, did his best to satisfy the
town's demands.

"I told them," he wrote in his diary that night, "that Capt Bruce
when he arrived would apply to the Body & that I would endeavor to
prevail on him to act with Reason in this Affair & that I was very sorry
he had any Tea on board—& which is very True for it hath given me
great uneasiness." He promised that he would notify the town officials
as soon as he learned of *Eleanor*'s arrival, and assured the meeting that
the tea aboard her would go back to England in her hold.

The crowd voted that Rowe's and Timmins's replies satisfied its
members.

Rowe then "staid some time at the Meeting & was Chose a Committee Man much against my will but I dare not say a word."

Quite late, John Copley returned, downcast, embarrassed, and nervous. He hoped, he began, that his listeners would excuse his tardy
arrival and "consider the difficulty of a passage by water at this season
as an apology." He had seen all the consignees, he said, and though he
had conveyed to them the meeting's assurance that they could come
before it with perfect safety, they had declined. It was their decision
that since they had been told that the meeting would accept nothing
less than the return of the tea, and since it was beyond their power to
reship it, they felt they could accomplish nothing by making a personal
appearance in Old South Church. They would, however, repeat their
promise to store the tea—and they offered a further concession: they
would allow it to be inspected at will by a town committee, to quiet
suspicions that it might be sneaked away and sold.

Here, at last, was the concession that John Scollay earlier surmised
would have ended the whole, grievous affair in agreeable compromise

if it had been offered at the start of the controversy. Instead, the consignees had frustrated the town's wishes for so long, the voters had lost all patience with them.

The congregation in Old South Church immediately passed a resolution that Copley's report was "not in the least degree satisfactory." It then branded any man "an enemy of the country" who tried to bring in tea from Britain while the Tea Act remained in force. Its members vowed to prevent the landing and sale of any tea so imported and to make certain that it was returned to Britain.

Copley had concluded his report by saying that it was the consensus of the consignees that "as they had not been active in introducing the tea, they would do nothing to obstruct the people in their procedure with the same." In other words, whatever happened from here on would be clearly the people's fault.

Many present suspected that with this ploy the consignees were merely acting as pawns of Governor Hutchinson's, and that the Governor had laid a devilish plan to place all the blame for the fate of the tea on the people of Boston. They gave Copley an angry grilling on this subject, as he reported the following day in a letter of rather uncertain spelling to Jonathan and Isaac Clarke:

> I made use of every argument my thoughts could suggest to draw the people from their unfavourable oppinion of you, and to convince them your opposition was neither the effect of obstinacy or unfriendliness to the community; . . . that you were uninfluanced by any persons what ever, that you had not seen the Governor that Day (this last I urged in answer to some very warm things that were said on this head in which You were charged with acting under the Imediate influance of the Governor which in justice to you and him I undertook to say from my own knowledg was not true. . . . I further observed that you had shewn no disposition to bring the Teas into the Town, nor would you; But only must be excused from being the Active instruments in sending it back. That the way was Clear for them to send it back by the Political Storm, as they termed it, raised by the Body . . . and that your refusal by no means frustrated their plan. In short I have done every possable thing, and altho there was a unanimous vote Declaring this unsattisfactory yet it cooled the Resentment and they Desolved without doing or saying any thing that showd an ill temper to you.

I have been told and I beleive it true, that after I left the Meeting Addams said they must not expect you should Ruin your selves.

Even as Copley wrote this last sentence, his belief in it faded, and he wrote in the margin, "This is doubtful." He was not without optimism for the outlook, however, as was apparent as the letter continued:

I think all stands well at present. Before the temper of the People could be judg'd of, we sent Cousin Harry to your Hon'd Father to urge his Imediate Departure to you. You will see him this Day. I have no doubt in my own mind you must stay where you are till the Vessel sails that is now in, at least; but I beleive not Longer; Then I think you will be able to return with Honour to Town, some few things in the mean while being done on your part. I had a Long and free conversation with Doc'r Warren, which will be renued this afternoon [Dec. 1st] with the addition of Col'l Hancock. Cousin Benj'n Davis is to be with us.

I must conclude with recommending that you avoid seeing the Govournor. I hope he will not have any occasion to go to the Castel; if he should do not converse with him on the subject. This, I think, is the best advise I can give boath as a friend to you and Him. . . .

X

On Tuesday morning, the second day of the big meeting, Captain Hall had brought *Dartmouth* up to Rowe's Wharf, where Rotch had obtained permission to anchor. Captain Proctor's guard sailed with him, and performed sentry duty all that day, reporting "all's well" at half-hour intervals while, as Mate Hodgdon duly noted in the ship's journal, the crew was "employed unbending the sails, getting out boats, etc."

That night, Proctor's guard was relieved in formal·ceremony by a fresh group of twenty-four volunteers, commanded by Ebenezer Cheever. This inaugurated a daily routine, which was maintained until the evening of December 16th.

During the cloudy morning of Wednesday, December 1st, Captain Hall ordered *Dartmouth* to be warped from Rowe's Wharf around to

nearby Griffin's, a process that consisted of moving the vessel by haul-
ing on its lines, looped around successive pilings along the route.

This move was presumably ordered by the Committee of Correspondence, by then in effectual charge of the town government. But *Dartmouth*'s log gives no hint of that. Mate Hodgdon merely recorded the
fact: "warped from Rowe's to Griffin's wharf; got out old junk and
moored ship—getting our sails and cables on shore." If the move was
dictated by the Committee of Correspondence, as historians have
judged, there was a good deal of justification for it: if all the incoming
tea ships were sent to the same wharf, a single company of guards could
easily keep watch over them. Furthermore, if trouble should develop,
defending forces could then be concentrated. Whatever the reason,
each tea ship as it entered the harbor was ordered to tie up at Griffin's
Wharf, which lay at the foot of Fort Hill, part of the harbor's southern
defenses.

Griffin's Wharf may simply have been more commodious than
Rowe's. Or Rowe, anticipating a ruckus and always anxious to avoid
unpleasantness with anyone, may have told Captain Hall to move
Dartmouth to Griffin's to make sure that a clash, if it did come,
wouldn't occur at his wharf. Griffin, whoever he was, apparently made
no objection.

By this time the little town of Boston was experiencing a crisis of
nerves.

Rumors flew that Admiral Montagu might send marines to over-
power *Dartmouth*'s guard and remove the tea to safer storage, or that
Colonel Leslie, however amiable by instinct, might turn nasty and dispatch soldiers for the same purpose. If either action should occur,
Mackintosh's "chickens" would certainly be rallied to oppose it. Perhaps even the Governor's Company of Cadets might join in the resistance.

John Andrews, a Boston merchant, noted in his diary on December
1st that one couldn't buy a pair of pistols anywhere in town, since they
had all been grabbed up by citizens "with a full determination to re-
pell force by force."

"My Heart beats at every Whistle I hear," wrote Abigail Adams to
her old friend Mercy Warren, "and I dare not openly express half my
fears." And, Mrs. John Adams was not easily frightened.

On the morning of December 2nd, tension was further tightened by
the arrival of John Rowe's vessel *Eleanor*. Rowe made terse mention

of it in his diary, but wrote nothing more until the following day. He then recorded that he and Captain Bruce had been summoned before the Committee of Correspondence. The Committee had ordered Bruce to proceed to Griffin's Wharf, and had given him the same instructions it had given Captain Hall: Don't land any of the tea. Take it back to Britain as soon as the rest of your cargo has been unloaded.

Both ships brought in many goods other than tea, and the Committee of Correspondence sensibly allowed those extraneous supplies, on which the merchants of Boston were depending for their winter business, to be taken off without hindrance. Mate Hodgdon wrote in *Dartmouth*'s log that he began discharging miscellaneous cargo, under the eyes of the guard, on December 2nd and continued to do so until Saturday, December 11th. By then *Dartmouth*'s hold had nothing left in it but tea—"that bainfull weed," as Abigail Adams called it.

Boston, though uneasy, seemed for a week to be relatively undivisive. John Rowe enjoyed a convivial evening with a mixed batch of Tories and Whigs at the Five Club on December 6th. On the following day he and Dr. Joseph Warren, in full masonic regalia of jewels and white aprons, were fellow-pallbearers at the burial of a lodge brother.

On December 8th the third teaship, Captain Hezekiah Coffin's *Beaver*, entered Nantasket Road, but in difficulty. Smallpox had broken out among the crew during the voyage. The harbor pilot ordered Captain Coffin to take his ship at once to Rainsford Island, the official quarantine station.

To the keeper of the hospital there, Boston's selectmen promptly sent a stern message. Their concern was not with smallpox, with which presumably the hospital was used to coping, but with the tea aboard *Beaver*.

"Our directions are," the message read, "that you take the whole of the tea from between decks upon the deck of the 'Briggandine.' If the weather be fair, let it lay on the deck the whole day, to be aired, and at night see it put between decks again; and you, with the true men you are ordered to take down with you, are to remain on board during the time the tea is on deck, and on no account to absent yourselves, and by no means suffer one chest of tea to be landed or taken away by any one. If any attempt should be made, you are immediately to dispatch a messenger to inform the selectmen thereof."

The Boston *Gazette*, in a flurry of puns, reported that Captain Coffin had arrived "not only with the Plague (TEA) on board, but also with the Small-Pox." It further commented, "As Tea is of a Drawing Quality, 'tis suspected it has suck'd in the Distemper; and therefore if permitted to be landed, 'tis presumed there would be no Purchaser."

Ordering the tea to be aired on deck all day long was only a sensible precaution to try to spare it from contamination during the smoking and other crude means of fumigation to which *Beaver*'s hold must be subjected before the vessel could be released from quarantine. Still, it would have taken a hardy soul to have purchased any of *Beaver*'s tea after the ceremonial exorcism of smallpox germs below decks.

On December 8th, Governor Hutchinson, determined not to let his opponents carry out their repeatedly avowed intentions, sent word to Admiral Montagu to be prepared to prevent any tea ship from leaving the harbor without official clearance. Montagu responded by shifting the positions of *Captain*, *Active*, and *Kingfisher* so that they blocked all feasible channels other than the main one, which lay securely under the guns of Castle William. (A British writer a few months later stated that this principal harbor fort—"strong, regular, well-built"—customarily mounted a hundred cannon.)

"The patriots now found themselves in a web of inextricable difficulties," wrote Thomas Hutchinson in 1774, when he was contemplating the recent past in British exile. It was curious that the Governor should then have called them "patriots," for in his view he was the true patriot; they were rebels.

The obstructive movements of the British vessels were observed in Boston, quite naturally, and inspired a letter of heavy sarcasm in the *Gazette*, signed by a writer using the preposterous pseudonym "Hononchrotonthologus," and mockingly stating:

To our utter astonishment, confusion, panick, distress, &c. &c. &c., we are advised by a gentleman trembling for the safety of the world that the terrific illustrious and most numerous armies now cooped up in Castle-William to countenance and protect the discomfited Tribe of Pensioners, Placemen, Commissioners and Consignees there resident have cleaned and loaded their muskets, have charged the cannon, even the 42-pounders; have stationed a large battalion on Governor's Island and planted artillery there; and that his Excellency the Hon. John Montague [Americans invariably misspelled it with an "e"], Rear Admiral of the Blue, has placed his formidable squadron with such address and thorough knowledge of naval operations as to alarm and terrify all Ameri-

cans. The universal consternation at these important movements
is past description, and the ladies are apprehensive that the musty
tea kindly conveyed to them from London will be crammed down
their throats with all expedition.

XI

Annoyance with Francis Rotch was growing, especially among the
members of the Boston Committee of Correspondence, for his apparent
failure to prepare to sail *Dartmouth* back to London with its forbidden
tea. True, the ship was being relieved of its other cargo, but the Committee knew that Rotch had not yet applied to the customs officials for
clearance to take his vessel out of the harbor.

Young Rotch had, however, been trying hard to squirm out of this
thoroughly awkward situation. It was not only turning many of his
fellow-townsmen against him but costing him a considerable sum of
money. Alongside Griffin's Wharf now lay the sloop *Triton*, with a
cargo of barreled whale oil. Rotch had contracted to transport the oil
to England in *Dartmouth* as soon as his ship was empty. He was
obliged to pay *Triton's* owners demurrage for every day their vessel
was prevented from discharging its cargo and departing on other
business. Also, each day that his own ship was unnecessarily detained
in port was a cause of financial loss to him. Besides, he had not been
able to collect from the consignees the freight charges due him for
bringing their tea to Boston.

In what proved to be a fruitless effort to resolve this impasse, Rotch
took Captain Hall and a notary public out to Castle William with him
on December 7th and "begged" the consignees to hand back the bill of
lading that Captain Hall had delivered to them upon arrival. Without
it, Rotch could not legally discharge his responsibility for the cargo.

With the notary carefully taking down every word, the consignees'
spokesman replied that in view of the mass meeting's resolutions on
November 29th and 30th that the tea should not be landed but be
returned, and further, in view of Rotch's own public promise to the
meeting to comply with its orders, and the fact that "there is continu-
ally on board your ship a number of armed men to prevent it being
landed," it was obviously "out of our power to receive it at present."

"But will you hand over the bill of lading and pay the freight charges due?" demanded Rotch. The charges amounted to ninety-seven pounds, seven shillings, and seven pence.

"We shall not deliver up Captain Hall's bill of lading, nor pay the freight of the teas until we can receive them," the notary recorded.

So much for that effort.

It seems as if Captain Hall must have told Captain Bruce of the *Eleanor* the story of this wasted pilgrimage, but Bruce, undeterred, made his own way out to Castle William with a notary four days later. The procedure was almost identical and the result was the same.

Captain Bruce, however, took the additional step of having his notary record a formal protest against the consignees, on his own behalf and John Rowe's, for all damages already suffered or that might thereafter be suffered "by their neglecting and refusing to receive, demand or take possession of the tea."

Meanwhile, on December 9th, Francis Rotch had undergone an uncomfortable session with the Committee of Correspondence. Why hadn't he asked the customs people for clearance to take his ship out of the harbor? the Committee demanded. Because, Rotch explained, in talking to a few of the customs men, he had become convinced there wasn't the slightest chance of obtaining it. Ask for it anyway, he was told, and if they won't grant it, make a formal protest.

Rotch was still temporizing two days later, when the Committee called him back. Samuel Adams, its chairman, was stern. "The ship must go," he said. "The people of Boston and the neighboring towns absolutely require and expect it."

Rotch was sufficiently troubled by this time to seek legal advice. He turned to the best lawyers he knew: John Adams and Sampson Salter Blowers, who, with Josiah Quincy, Jr., had valiantly undertaken the unpopular defense of the British soldiers unjustly accused of murder at the time of the Boston Massacre. Once again John Adams was obliged by his knowledge of the law and his strict sense of justice to make a decision that wouldn't please the hotly rebellious element of his townsmen. He joined with Blowers, a royalist, in advising Rotch to defy the Committee of Correspondence and refuse to take his ship out of the harbor without an official clearance. If Rotch were to obey the Committee, his lawyers told him, his ship at least would be confiscated; at worst it might be blown out of the water by British guns, even if the shots were intended only as warnings.

Public pressure on Rotch was intensified by the newspapers, espe-

cially by the *Gazette,* which on December 13th declared, "If Mr. Rotch
the Owner of Captain Hall's Ship does not intend she shall depart
DIRECTLY with the Tea she bro't, he ought explicitly to declare it, that
the People may know what to depend upon and how to conduct themselves. It does not appear that she is yet in Readiness, or that he has
even made a Demand at the Custom-House for a Clearance. The Minds
of the Publick are greatly irritated at his Delay hitherto to take this
necessary Step towards complying with their PEREMPTORY REQUISITION."

At the same time the *Gazette,* doubtless at Samuel Adams's instigation, stiffened public resolve by printing a sharply needling letter from
Philadelphia, which said, in part: "Our Tea Consignees have all resign'd, and you need not fear; the Tea will not be landed here or at
New-York. All that we fear is that you will shrink at Boston. You have
fail'd us in the Importation of Tea from London since the Non-importation Agreement, and we fear you will suffer this to be landed. . . .
May God give you Virtue enough to save the Liberties of your Country . . . ."

XII

It was on this thirteenth day of December that plans are believed to
have been made for the destruction of the tea, if all efforts failed to dispose of it by other means. The Committees of Correspondence of Cambridge, Charlestown, Dorchester, and Roxbury—Boston's four nearest
neighbors—met with the local Committee of twenty-one members in
an all-day session at Faneuil Hall. The proceedings were intensive but
secret. They began early and lasted until late evening. Yet the minutes
merely stated, "No business transacted matter of record." Undoubtedly,
though, those long hours of discussion produced the strategy for the
three days remaining before the legal deadline for *Dartmouth*'s cargo
to escape confiscation by the customs authorities. That deadline was
midnight on December 16th, and the word was already going around
that after that hour the customs men wouldn't let even a minute pass
before seizing the ship's chests of tea, and those on the adjacent vessels.

As a result of the secret meeting at Faneuil Hall, fresh handbills were
up all over Boston before dawn on December 14th. They read:

> Friends! Brethren! Countrymen! The perfidious act of your
> reckless enemies to render ineffectual the late resolves of the body

of the people demands your assembling at the Old South Meeting House precisely at ten o'clock this day, at which time the bells will ring.

A large crowd gathered at the appointed hour. Samuel Phillips Savage, former Boston selectman and present father-in-law of Henry Bass, a member of the secret, militant Loyal Nine, was elected moderator of the meeting.

The first order of business was to summon Captain Bruce of the *Eleanor* and demand his promise to ask the customs officials at once to clear his ship for London. Bruce, barely restraining a notorious temper and his strong distaste for anti-royalist activities, grudgingly agreed.

"If I'm refused, though," he remarked querulously, "I'm loath to stand the shot of thirty-two pounders from the Castle."

He was dismissed, and thoroughly harassed Francis Rotch was recalled.

Rotch was then obliged to confess, in effect before the whole town, that he had not yet applied for *Dartmouth*'s clearance; that his lawyers had warned him that to take his ship out without it would risk its seizure and his consequent ruin. Therefore, he said, he was obliged to rescind his promise, exacted at an earlier meeting against his will, to carry *Dartmouth*'s tea back to Britain.

Speakers at the meeting, not entirely lacking sympathy for his position, then persuaded him at least to apply for clearance. They would send a committee of ten with him, to lend weight to his mission and bear witness to the customs official's reply. The audience in Old South Meeting House was assured that the emissaries would report to them before the day was done.

The escorting committee, headed by Samuel Adams, conducted Rotch to the customhouse. There they were dubiously received by Richard Harrison, a customs collector who had been viciously manhandled by a hostile Boston mob five years earlier in the performance of his duty and was therefore not predisposed to be indulgent in construing regulations. Harrison said he couldn't decide how to respond to Rotch's request without consulting his superior, Robert Hallowell, comptroller of customs for North America. Hallowell was out at the moment. Harrison could only say that the two would confer on the matter and be ready to give the delegation their answer the following morning.

Adams and his little band returned to Old South Church with their

Governor Hutchinson's country home on Milton Hill with superb views both toward the sea and toward Worcester and where Hutchinson "holed up" for a good portion of the period leading up to the Boston Tea Party.

disappointing report, and the meeting was adjourned until Thursday, December 16th, the day of crucial decision.

XIII

While these events were transpiring, Governor Hutchinson had been brooding in Milton over the news brought to him that another mass meeting had gathered in Boston. He had been sufficiently stirred by the tidings to write another letter to Lord Dartmouth, his chief, on the heels of one that had declared that if only Boston could somehow be separated from the rest of the Province, "I think my government would be very easy to me." Now Boston was badly misbehaving again, and Hutchinson in his exasperation thought he saw the outline of a possible solution.

"It would be a good measure," he wrote to Lord Dartmouth on December 14th, "if the General Court could be brought to the enacting [of] a law for disfranchising such towns as assemble for other purposes than the immediate concern of the town. . . . It looks as if the principal actors in some late Town-Meetings were afraid of being, at one time or other, called to account by some other authority than any within the Province; for when anything very extravagant is to be done, a meeting of the people at large is called by printed notification, without signing; but selectmen, town clerk, etc., attend. In the last assembly in the largest meeting-house in town, a gent who spoke in behalf of the consignees called upon the selectmen. Mr. Adams [Samuel], the representative [in the General Court], corrected him and remarked that they knew no selectmen at those meetings. Surely, my Lord, it is time this anarchy was restrained and corrected by some authority or other."

Hutchinson must have felt especially sanguine in addressing his suggestions for changes in governmental policy to Lord Dartmouth. The Secretary of State for the American Department was no mere functionary, far down the pyramid of officialdom. Dartmouth was the beloved step-brother of Lord Frederick North, the Prime Minister, who in turn had been a cherished friend of King George III's since they were boys together, in the days when Lord North's father was the King's tutor. Hutchinson's letters were certain to receive attention.

On the same day that the Governor was calling for an end to Boston's "anarchy," his eldest son, Tom—"in exile," as he described it—was

writing a chatty note to Billy, the youngest, in Middleborough.
"I imagine," he began, "you are anxious to know what the poor
banished Consignees are doing at the Castle," and then it continued:

> Our retreat here was sudden, but our enemies do not say we
> came too soon. How long we shall be imprisoned 'tis impossible
> to say. I am glad for your sake you can remain in quiet where
> you are.
>
> The proceedings of the people, while assembled, you have in
> print. We have since had application from the owners and masters
> of the vessels to receive the teas, who at the same time acknowl-
> edged 25 armed men were watching the vessels to prevent it.
> However, they have protested against us. I suppose they have taken
> this step more to serve themselves than to hurt us; but being
> surrounded with cannon, we have [given?] them such answers as
> we shou'd not have dared to do in any other situation.
>
> I hear there is a meeting of the mob-ility today, but don't know
> the result. I hardly think they will attempt sending the tea back;
> but am more sure it will not go many leagues. . . .
>
> . . . we are as comfortable as we can be in a very cold place,
> driven from our family's & business, with the months of January
> and February just at hand. I hear you have been to Milton, tho'
> I suppose you are quite safe where you are: yet it's best to keep
> close till the infernal spirit is lay'd, or at least cool'd. . . .
>
> P.S. Our situation is rendered more agreeable by the polite
> reception we met with from Col. Leslie and the other gentlemen of
> the army. At present I think I shall not speedily return to Boston
> if allowed to quit this place.

On December 15th, the brig *Beaver* was released from quarantine
and directed to proceed to Griffin's Wharf, which it did.

In the course of the same day, Samuel Adams received urgent word
from the Plymouth Committee of Correspondence that the fourth tea
ship, the Clarkes' pokey brig *William*, would never arrive. It had been
driven aground in a gale the previous Friday "on the back of Cape
Cod." The news came by courier. It disclosed that the vessel was a ruin,
but that its cargo, including fifty-eight chests of tea and three hundred
street lamps for Boston, was salvageable.

Adams replied at once, utilizing the same courier, and urging
prompt action to prevent the tea from reaching the consignees. He

also sent a letter to the Sandwich Committee of Correspondence, urging them to help their Plymouth neighbors in this effort.

But somehow the news of the wreck had found its way behind the walls of Castle William at about the same time. Jonathan Clarke had slipped out to make his lonely, dangerous way to the Cape, find the wrecked brig's captain, Joseph Loring, and make hasty arrangements for transferring the cargo to a lighter that would transport it to well-guarded storage at the Castle. He succeeded in his venture, much to the anger and disgust of Sam Adams, when he found out about it.

At the beginning of customhouse office hours on December 15th, Francis Rotch and his ten unwelcome companions from Tuesday's mass meeting paid a return visit to Collector Harrison. Both Harrison and Comptroller Hallowell were waiting for them. The meeting was brief and cold.

Rotch rather flusteredly explained that he was asking for clearance for *Dartmouth* only because he was compelled to. Harrison gave a stiffly formal reply, telling everyone in the room what they already knew: the ship carried dutiable goods, on which the required duty had not been paid. Therefore, "it is impossible for me to grant you any clearance for her whatever," Harrison declared, "it being utterly inconsistent with my duty."

The delegation departed in icy silence, but Adams saw to it that Rotch also paid a call on the Navy officer who had authority to give outbound vessels a permit to pass Castle William once they had cleared customs. Naturally the officer refused to give him the requested permit.

The only recourse left was an appeal to Governor Hutchinson. That was planned for Thursday. Adams was obviously taking great pains to make sure that all formalities were observed, so that the record would show that he and the others who opposed dutied tea had done all they could to dispose of the tea legally and yet not comply with the Tea Act.

XIV

On Thursday, December 16th, at ten o'clock in the morning, more people had assembled at Old South Meeting House than had ever before come together at one place in Boston. There were, in fact, far more people than the cavernous church would hold. Contemporary estimates placed the crowd at seven thousand persons, at least two thousand of whom had come in from nearby towns.

The day was rainy and cold, but those who could not find room to sit or stand in the church persisted in hanging around its entrance doors on broad Marlborough Street, ignoring the grim weather in their eagerness not to miss a moment of what everyone knew would be a memorable day. No handbills had been posted, no bells rung. Yet the countryside for twenty miles around was in a ferment of excitement over the knowledge that this day afforded the last chance to dispatch the dutiable tea on its retreat to London, and many from outside had flocked to town to witness the outcome. One delegation had even traveled down from Lebanon, Maine.

The committee that had accompanied Francis Rotch on his fruitless mission of the previous day reported at the start of the meeting. Rotch was then told that the people expected him to protest officially to the comptroller of customs that he had been denied clearance for *Dartmouth*. More importantly, he must leave for Milton at once and ask the Governor to grant him a permit to enable his vessel to pass the fort on Castle Island. Finally, he was ordered to prepare *Dartmouth* to set sail for London before midnight. Would he comply?

"Gentlemen, I cannot," replied Rotch. "It is wholly impracticable. It would cause my ruin."

Another speaker reminded him of his earlier promise to take *Dartmouth* out of the harbor within twenty days of the ship's arrival. Today was the twentieth day. "Will you order your vessel to sail this day?"

"No," answered Rotch, whose mild Quaker demeanor cloaked a steely stubbornness. "I will not. I cannot."

There was nothing punitive to be done about his refusal on this point. But he was told to delay no longer in protesting to customs or in setting out to seek a permit from the Governor. He was given until three o'clock in the afternoon to accomplish his errand. It involved a round trip of about fifteen miles on horseback over frozen, rutty roads in addition to the time he would need at Milton.

The meeting was then adjourned until three, with no one in any doubt about what the Governor's answer would be.

Rotch gloomily rode his horse through the dark day to the broad crest of Milton Hill, where Hutchinson's low, spacious Georgian summer residence stood, on a gently sloping ridge from which he could look to the Blue Hills in the west and across the Neponset River marshes to the islands of Boston Harbor in the east. It was the Governor's favorite home, where he had spent twenty summers and to which he had now retreated from possibly rough contact with the "mob-ility."

Hutchinson greeted his young caller, whom he well knew, with friendly dignity. Rotch began his remarks with an apology. He had come, he said, to beg the Governor to issue a pass for his ship, since the customhouse had refused it clearance. But he was there against his will, he hurried to explain, "and because I am compelled to it."

Describing the subsequent conversation afterward in a letter to Israel Mauduit, a political agent for the Massachusetts House of Representatives in London, the Governor remarked, "The pass you will easily suppose I did not grant."

"I told him," wrote Hutchinson, "that when his vessel was regularly cleared out, and not before, he should have a pass. I asked him what he imagined the intentions of the people to be with respect to the tea. He said he had always supposed they had no other intention than forcing it back to England, and he believed they wished to have the vessel go down and be stopped by a shot from the Castle, that they might say that they had done all in their power.

"I had heard that some persons had that day advised him to haul his ship from the wharf into the stream, and I offered him a letter to the Admiral, recommending ship and goods to his protection." By this time the Governor had evidently decided that the Castle was the safest place for the tea as well as the consignees.

"He said he had been so advised," continued Hutchinson in his letter to Mauduit, "but could not get hands, and should have made himself obnoxious to the people by doing it, or by applying to the Admiral. He was under no concern about his ship—the rage was against the tea."

So the short interview ended.

The sun had set at about half-past four, and Rotch began his return journey in the dark. The rain had stopped and the sky was clearing, but with the end of the storm came a fresh northwest wind and a sharper chill than ever. There was a thin moon midway down the western sky, but being only three days old, it gave no discernible illumination for travelers.

While Rotch was gone, the huge crowd had poured back into Old

South Meeting House at three o'clock. They had then listened to an hour and a half of oratory from Samuel Adams, Dr. Joseph Warren, and Josiah Quincy, Jr. The last, already mortally ill with tuberculosis at the age of twenty-seven, was not only the youngest of the speakers but the most brilliant—and, surprisingly, the most cautionary.

His cheeks flushed with excitement and fever, young Quincy solemnly warned:

> It is not, Mr. Moderator, the spirit that vapors within these walls that must stand us in stead. The exertions of this day will call forth the events which will make a very different spirit necessary for our salvation. Whoever supposes that shouts and hosannas will terminate the trials of the day entertains a childish fancy. We must be grossly ignorant of the importance and value of the prize for which we contend; we must be equally ignorant of the power of those who have combined against us; we must be blind to that malice, inveteracy, and insatiable revenge which actuates our enemies, public and private, abroad and in our bosom, to hope that we shall end this controversy without the sharpest—the sharpest—conflicts; to flatter ourselves that popular resolves, popular harangues, popular acclamations, and popular vapor will vanquish our foes.
>
> Let us consider the issue. Let us look to the end. Let us weigh and consider before we advance to those measures which must bring on the most trying and terrific struggle this country ever saw.

Quincy quite obviously knew what was brewing for that evening. So did a good many others present. And his thoughtful warning was brushed aside by an audience impatient to bring matters to a dramatic conclusion.

When darkness fell, and the church's clustered candles were lighted, Rotch had still not returned. Many suspected that. he had no intention of doing so. Several motions were made to adjourn the meeting. Protests against this maneuver came mainly from out-of-towners, one of whom rose to declare that "Mr. Rotch has been seen on his way to Milton, and there is no reason to doubt his good faith. Besides, our several towns are so very anxious to have full information as to this matter that they are quite desirous the meeting should be continued until six o'clock." Motions to adjourn were overruled.

All of a sudden, Francis Rotch appeared at one of the entrance doors, and in the flickering light from the chandeliers made his way through the excited crowd to a position in front of the moderator.

There was a tense hush as Samuel Savage asked him the result of his visit with the Governor.

"His Excellency told me he was willing to grant anything consistent with the laws and his duty to the King," Rotch reported, "but that he could not give a pass unless the vessel was properly qualified from the Customs House. But, provided she was properly cleared, he would make no distinction between my vessel and any other."

"Did you present your protest to the Customs House?" Rotch was asked.

"I had no time to finish it before leaving for Milton," he replied, "so I could not carry it with me to the Governor, but I told him what steps I had already taken and what I intended to do about the protest."

"Will you send your vessel back with the tea in her under these present circumstances?" Moderator Savage asked.

"I cannot possibly do so," said Rotch. "It would prove my ruin."

"Do you have any intention of landing the tea?"

"I have no business doing so," Rotch answered, "but if I were called upon to do so by the proper persons, I would try to land it for my own security's sake."

At this point, an impetuous man in the audience shouted, "Who knows how tea will mingle with sea water?"

[For years this shouted question was attributed to timid John Rowe, the least likely person to have uttered it. In due time, with the publication of his diary, firm evidence became available that he could not have said it. His diary entry for December 16th began, "I being a little Unwell staid at home all Day & all the evening." Rowe did not bother to explain whether his illness was physical or diplomatic, but it was probably genuine, for he was still remaining indoors the next morning.]

The crowd broke into cheers. There were a few yells for "A mob! A mob!"

Moderator Savage hammered on the rostrum with his gavel and commanded silence.

Dr. Thomas Young, an effective speaker, told the audience that Mr. Rotch was a good man, who had done his best to satisfy them. No one, he said, should attempt to harm him or his property.

Samuel Adams then stood up and declared, with a gesture of hopelessness and resignation, "This meeting can do nothing more to save the country."

Since Adams's voice was weak and shaky, his words were probably not heard farther than six pews away, but his gesture, presumably agreed upon in advance, could be seen from the front entrance. There, as if by prearrangement, immediately sounded a howling chorus of warwhoops. These were echoed by men standing in the back of the church balcony.

Someone shouted, "Boston Harbor a teapot tonight!" Another yelled, "Hurrah for Griffin's Wharf!"

Again Samuel Savage noisily banged the rostrum until the uproar quieted. He then read a prepared motion. Since the people, he said, "having manifested exemplary patience and caution," had done everything possible to preserve the East India Company's tea, and yet not allow duty to be paid on it or permit it to be sold; and since they had endeavored in every way to have it sent back unharmed to its owners, though obstructed every step of the way by the consignees "and their coadjutors"—there was nothing left for this meeting to do but adjourn.

The audience responded with a roar of approval and began pushing strenuously toward the doors.

John Andrews, who lived near by, later wrote in his journal, with a brief indulgence in private bravado, that he was "drinking tea at home" when the first cheers and warwhoops resounded. He was so curious that he immediately went over to the church and tried to find out what was going on.

Andrews had been unable to get farther than the porch of Old South "when I found the Moderator was just declaring the meeting to be *dissolv'd,* which caused another great shout, out doors and in, and three cheers.

"What with that, and the consequent noise of breaking up the meeting," he commented, "you'd thought that the inhabitants of the infernal regions had broke loose."

Mingling Tea with Sea Water

(December 16, 1773: 6–9 P.M.)

But, BEHOLD, what followed! A number of brave & resolute men, determined to do all in their power to save their country from the ruin which their enemies had plotted, in less than four hours emptied every chest of tea on board the three ships commanded by the captains Hall, Bruce, and Coffin, amounting to 342 chests, into the sea! ! without the least damage done to the ships or any other property.

—The Boston *Gazette*, Monday, December 20, 1773.

I

As the tumultuous crowd burst through the doors of Old South Meeting House a few minutes before six o'clock that night, those in the forefront saw and heard a bizarre-looking little group of men hurrying down Milk Street toward the harbor, howling like savages.

"They say the actors were *Indians* from *Narragansett*," wrote John Andrews, who knew perfectly well that they weren't. From his last-minute position on the church porch, Andrews had had a chance to look these men over briefly at close range. He described them well in a tongue-in-cheek letter written two days later to a friend in Philadelphia:

Whether they were or not, to a transient observer they appear'd as *such*, being cloath'd in Blankets with the heads muffled, and

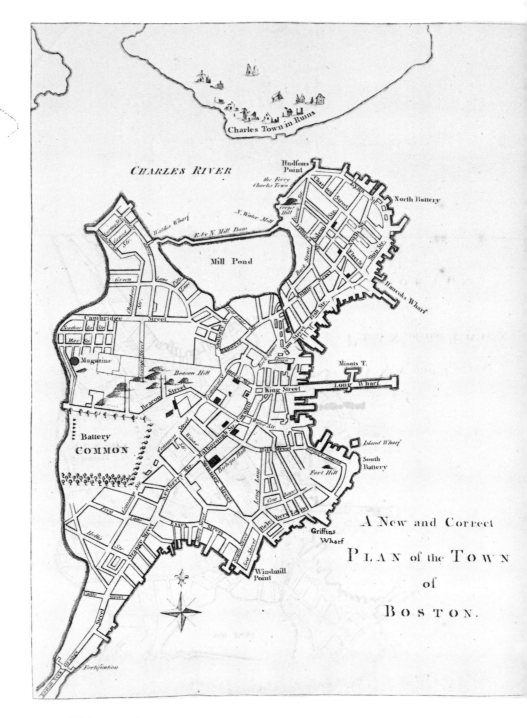

This map of Boston, made while the British were still *in situ,* shows most locations of interest to followers of this Boston Tea Party narrative.

copper color'd countenances, being each arm'd with a hatchet or axe, and pair of pistols, nor was their *dialect* different from which I conceive these geniuses to *speak*, as their jargon was unintelligible to all but themselves.

Hundreds who had streamed out of the church ran after these "Indians," well aware that they were fellow-townsmen in prudent disguise, though unable to identify any of them. That, of course, was the point of the disguise—so that no witness could ever give positive testimony.

The masqueraders soon swerved off Milk Street into Hutchinson Street, which led straight southeastward, past Fort Hill and across a couple of lanes, to Griffin's Wharf.

Alexander Hodgdon, *Dartmouth*'s mate, recorded in the ship's journal with his customary sporadic underscoring what happened next.

> Between six and seven o'clock this evening came down to the wharf a body of about *one thousand people.* Among them were a number *dressed and whooping like Indians.* They came on board the ship, and after warning myself and the Custom-House officer to get out of the way, they unlaid the hatches and went down the hold, where was eighty whole and thirty-four half chests of Tea, which they hoisted upon deck, and cut the chests to pieces, and hove the Tea all overboard, where it was damaged and lost.

The Boston Tea Party had begun. It lasted approximately three hours and, from the viewpoint of Samuel Adams and his numerous followers, was a complete success. By the time it was over, every ounce of tea that the East India Company had consigned to Boston on the *Dartmouth, Eleanor* and *Beaver* had been scattered upon the harbor waters, except for a few shreds accidentally carried off in raiders' shoes.

[The fact that the action had, in effect, begun the American Revolution and would lead, as Josiah Quincy, Jr., had predicted, to "the most trying and terrific struggle" that the colonies had ever seen had no dampening effect upon those enjoying the gutty satisfaction of striking a heavy, unexpected, but bloodless blow against a despised government. Few foresaw the consequences, nor would they likely have been deterred if they had.

The significance of the events set in train that evening was better

realized three years later, when an anonymous New Hampshire poet
wrote these rueful lines:

> What discontents, what dire events,
> From trifling things proceed?
> A little Tea, thrown in the sea,
> Has thousands caused to bleed.]

The raiders were predominantly young. Only seven of them were
over forty. Of those whose age at the time could later be determined,
sixteen were in their thirties, thirty-eight were in their twenties, and
fifteen were teen-agers. The youngest contingent consisted entirely of
apprentices. They had not been taken into consideration when the
plans were being laid. Unable to resist the allure of whistles and warwhoops in the street, they simply joined the Party on the spur of the
moment, for a lark. Most of them were not disguised. Indeed, many of
the older men were only partially so, having done no more than dis-
color their faces.

The decision had apparently been made at the secret session of the
Committees of Correspondence from five towns held in Faneuil Hall
on December 13th to have three groups of men, including the leaders
of the raid, don makeshift Indian attire for the occasion. It was truly
crude disguise, consisting mostly of ragged clothes, any sort of hood for
the head and shoulders, and some obscuring color for the face and
hands. Headgear included blankets, shawls, cast-off dresses, and red
woolen caps. Skin colors ranged from red ochre, through a mixture of
that pigment with lampblack and axle grease, to pure soot. If anyone
wore a feathered headband, no contemporary account mentioned it.

The three groups assembled in separate parts of town and began
putting on their costumes and makeup during the short afternoon of
December 16th, while the impatient audience in Old South Church
was fretting through oratory. By dark, they were ready to make their
way to a designated rendezvous on Fort Hill, with one group stopping
off at Old South Meeting House en route.

[Why the raiders chose to pretend to be Indians is not known, though
in America in 1773 the thought of a raid instinctively evoked a mental
image of Indians. Disguise of some sort was thought to be advisable
for self-protection, and there were precedents in Boston for dressing up

for deviltry. The costumed imps who frolicked about the Pope's Day processions and engaged in the subsequent street brawls always painted their faces. And when feeling ran particularly high against British tax collectors in 1768 and 1770, hoodlums who harassed them and sometimes damaged their houses resorted to "most hideous howlings, as the Indians," Ann Hulton reported. When, in the middle of a June night in 1770, a band of ruffians had marched out into the country from Boston and smashed all the windows in her brother's house, they had blackened their faces for the deed, and wore white nightcaps and white stockings. Some of those valiants probably joined more respectable citizens in staging the Tea Party.]

One group began their preparations for the derring-do of December 16, 1773, in Benjamin Edes's parlor before the sun went down. The printer's son Peter, only a lad but old enough to mix rum punch, was assigned the chore of keeping the festive bowl filled. This he did in an adjoining room. The parlor door was closed. Peter could hear "a number of gentlemen" gathering there, but "I was not admitted to their presence, for fear, I suppose, of their being known," he told his own son long afterward. Benjamin Edes emerged to fetch more punch whenever it was needed. All Peter knew was that the exertions of the gentlemen next door required him to refill the punch bowl several times. Doubtless this particular group of raiders uttered the most fearsome war whoops when the time came, and were inspired to try to talk like Indians as well as look like them.

At dusk, in another part of town, Joseph Levering, fifteen, held high a whale-oil lantern while more than a dozen men in John Crane's carpentry shop put on outlandish garb and painted their faces and hands.

Not all the "Indians" prepared for the raid in groups. Benjamin Russell, who was then a schoolboy, later remembered peeping through a window in the family woodshed late that afternoon and seeing his father, a young mason, and Thomas Moore, who operated a commercial wharf, busily applying burnt cork to each other's cheeks and chortling at the results.

Amos Lincoln, still an apprentice at the age of twenty, had his master's help in getting ready for the evening's adventure. His master, a devout man named Crafts, was strongly in sympathy with those who opposed landing the dutiable tea, but had no intention of joining them

in destroying it. Instead, that afternoon, he rounded up a costume of
sorts for Amos, helped him into it, and blackened his face and hands.
He then dropped to his knees beside the apprentice and "prayed most
fervently that he [Amos] might be protected in the enterprise in which
he was engaged."

Peter Slater, fourteen, the youngest person to take part in the raid,
was one of the baker's dozen of apprentices who invited themselves
to the Party. Peter was apprenticed to a ropemaker, who was going to
be a participant himself but thought it judicious to lock Peter in
his room before the Party began. The apprentice climbed out a window when he heard the uproar in the street. He ran into a nearby
blacksmith's shop, and there found the owner applying the final touches
to his disguise. The latter indulgently advised Peter to tie a bandanna
around his head and rub his face with charcoal. He then took the lad
along with him to the raid. Twenty other persons joined them as they
made their way to Griffin's Wharf.

Those who had planned the Boston Tea Party had evidently intended
that the participants should make their way as unobtrusively as possible to Fort Hill after dark, and move in a body from there.

Two of the raiders, hurrying to Fort Hill by themselves, were said
to have encountered a British officer. It seems improbable that he
would have been permitted to venture into Boston from the Castle
after dark when the town was known to be in the grip of angry excitement, largely anti-British, but William Tudor told the story, and
Tudor, then a law student in John Adams's office, was presumably a
reliable source.

According to Tudor, the officer, startled at the sight of two "Indians"
approaching him along a footpath, lighting their way with a lantern,
drew his sword. In response, one of the raiders pulled out a pistol,
and said coolly, "The path is wide enough for us all. We have nothing
to do with you, and intend you no harm. If you keep your own way
peaceably, we shall keep ours."

There Tudor's story ended.

John Andrews wrote that Fort Hill was the designated place of assembly, and that the raiders mustered there, he had been told, "to
the number of about two hundred, and proceeded, two by two, to
Griffin's Wharf." Andrews appears to have exaggerated both the numbers and the discipline, though militia officers were in charge and may

possibly have ordered their grotesque troops to march down Fort Hill in a column of twos to attack the tea chests.

If such incongruous discipline prevailed at Fort Hill, it was lacking elsewhere, for the raiders received impromptu reinforcements from the rapidly gathering crowd of witnesses as they began their work.

One of these impulsive helpers, Robert Sessions, writing in his old age, provided particularly vivid recollections of the scene:

> I was living in Boston at the time, in the family of a Mr. Davis, a lumber merchant, as a common laborer. On that eventful evening, when Mr. Davis came in from the town meeting, I asked him what was to be done with the tea.
>
> "They are now throwing it overboard," he replied.
>
> Receiving permission, I went immediately to the spot. Everything was as light as day, by the means of lamps and torches; a pin might be seen lying on the wharf. I went on board where they were at work, and took hold with my own hands.
>
> I was not one of those appointed to destroy the tea, and who disguised themselves as Indians, but was a volunteer, the disguised men being largely men of family and position in Boston, while I was a young man whose home and relations were in Connecticut. The appointed and disguised party proving too small for the quick work necessary, other young men, similarly circumstanced with myself, joined them in their labors.
>
> The chests were drawn up by a tackle—one man bringing them forward [in the hold], another putting a rope around them, and others hoisting them to the deck and carrying them to the vessel's side. The chests were then opened, the tea emptied over the side, and the chests thrown overboard.
>
> Perfect regularity prevailed during the whole transaction. Although there were many people on the wharf, entire silence prevailed—no clamor, no talking. Nothing was meddled with but the teas on board.
>
> After having emptied the whole, the deck was swept clean, and everything put in its proper place. An officer on board was requested to come up from the cabin and see that no damage was done except to the tea.

[Another stray swept into the Tea Party was Samuel Sprague, nine-teen, a mason's apprentice who was on his way to a date with the girl he later married when "I met some lads hurrying along towards Grif-fin's Wharf, who told me there was something going on there. I joined them, and on reaching the wharf found the 'Indians' busy with the tea chests.

"Wishing to have my share of the fun," he wrote long years later, "I looked about for some means of disguising myself. Spying a low building with a stovepipe by way of a chimney, I climbed the roof and obtained a quantity of soot, with which I blackened my face.

"Joining the party, I recognized among them Mr. Etheridge, my master. We worked together, but neither of us ever afterwards alluded to each other's share in the proceedings."]

The strange quiet that prevailed, except for the sound of ripping tea chests and numerous splashes in the water, made a lasting impres-sion upon several witnesses.

One of them was Dr. Hugh Williamson of Philadelphia, a leading advocate of American independence and a close friend of Benjamin Franklin's. Williamson had been in Boston for a month on business and was about to take ship for London. He had attended at least two of the large public meetings that preceded the Tea Party, and when he heard on the night of December 16th that the Party was in progress, he went at once to the scene. He found a little hummock about fifty yards from the nearest ship and, standing there, enjoyed a clear view of the proceedings.

"The rioters made very little noise," he told the King's Council, in wonderfully self-contradictory phraseology, a few months later.

At least one sizable contingent of apprentices and journeymen, numbering close to thirty, acted without apparent coordination with the more disciplined raiders from Fort Hill and evidently with only superficial knowledge of their intentions. In fact, they appear to have arrived first on the scene, unbriefed.

One of them, Joshua Wyeth, recalled that "we first talked of firing the ships, but feared the fire would communicate to the town. We then proposed sinking them [indicating a lack of knowledge on their part of how shallow the water was in that vicinity], but dropped the project through fear that we should alarm the town before we could get through with it.

"We had observed," he continued "that very few persons remained on board the ships, and we finally concluded that we could take possession of them, and discharge the tea into the harbor without danger or opposition."

They donned old clothes and smeared their faces with lampblack and grease until they "should not have known each other except by our voices. Our most intimate friends among the spectators had not the least knowledge of us. We surely resembled devils from the bottomless pit rather than men."

"At an appointed time," his account went on, "we met in an old building at the head of the wharf, and then fell in one after another, as if by accident, so as not to excite suspicion.

"We placed a sentry at the head of the wharf, another in the middle, and one on the bow of each ship as we took possession. . . . Our sentries were not armed, and could not stop any who insisted on passing. They were particularly charged to give us notice in case any known Tory came down to the wharf."

Ebenezer Stevens was with the group of grog-fueled raiders whose war whoops had broken up the meeting at Old South Church. He remembered in later years that *Dartmouth* was their first target (as contemporary newspapers confirmed), and that the tea ships' guard that night consisted of members of his own militia company of Paddock's Artillery. The guard immediately joined the raiders in plundering the tea.

Stevens had to back off *Dartmouth*, however, when he discovered that Mate Hodgdon was on board. Hodgdon was an acquaintance, and Stevens was afraid to run even an outside chance of his being recognized. So "I left that vessel with some of my comrades and went aboard another vessel, which lay at the opposite side of the wharf. Numbers of others took our places on board Hodgdon's vessel."

One of them was Josh Wyeth, who recalled that "our leader, in a very stern and resolute manner, ordered the captain and crew to open the hatchways and hand us the hoisting tackle and ropes, assuring them that no harm was intended them. The captain asked what we intended to do. Our leader told him that we were going to unload the tea, and ordered him and his crew below. They instantly obeyed."

The raiders then went about their business.

Word of what was happening at Griffin's Wharf flashed across town. Troops at the Castle were put on alert, but individual members of

Two artists' views of the Boston Tea Party dating from the 1880's. The top view done in 1884, takes a rather fanciful perspective. The bottom, done in 1881, offers a more literal rendition.

the Governor's Council sent urgent messages to Colonel Leslie that they must not be sent into town. That would risk a far greater blood-letting than had occurred in the clash between troops and townspeople three years earlier, at the time of the Boston Massacre.

There was a brief delay at the brig, *Beaver*. Captain Coffin, who hadn't been able to do much unloading since his late arrival on December 13th, protested to the raiders that the tea aboard was covered with layers of goods belonging to various merchants in town. He urged them to give him time to finish discharging the inoffensive portion of the cargo before they tackled the tea.

Their leader brushed him aside. "The tea we want and the tea we'll have," he said. "If you'll go to your cabin quietly, not one article of your goods will be hurt."

Coffin subsided. The raiders carefully unloaded every item of miscellaneous cargo and then happily smashed up the tea chests.

No damage was done to any of the ships, except for the busting of a single padlock, which was replaced anonymously the following day.

[The sole human casualty was John Crane, twenty-nine, the carpenter in whose shop one of the three main bodies of raiders had prepared for the evening. A hoist being used to haul tea chests up on deck suddenly collapsed under an excessive load and struck Crane in falling. He was knocked senseless. A few companions, thinking he had been killed and not wanting to leave their urgent assignment any longer than necessary, hastily carried him off the wharf into a woodworking shop near by. There they laid him on the floor and hid his body under a pile of shavings. Later in the evening, when the raid was over and the neighborhood was empty and silent, they crept back to recover the body, only to find Crane dizzily sitting up, sick, dazed with pain, but indubitably alive. He recovered.]

II

Two unforeseen complications hampered and delayed the work of destruction that evening. The tea chests were sheathed in canvas, which blunted the strokes of axes and hatchets, some of which were doubtless in need of sharpening anyway. And there was little water in which to dispose of the debris, once the wreckers had succeeded in breaking open the chests. Even at high tide, the depth of the harbor in the vicinity of Griffin's Wharf rarely exceeded six feet. At low tide, it was closer to two feet.

Ideally, the Tea Party should have taken place just past the tide peak, when the water was deepest but beginning to ebb, so that its steady outward movement would have carried the loose tea away from shore. But high tide that night did not occur until two hours after midnight, and the customs men were known to be waiting to pounce on the tea chests if they were still aboard the ships at midnight.

Prodded by necessity, the "Indians" descended on the ships when the tide was close to dead low, and still ebbing. The vessels themselves were squatting in the muck of the bottom. The water around them was so shallow that the tea flung overboard rapidly heaped up like stacks of hay. At least one stack grew so tall it toppled over onto the deck from which it had been thrown. Apprentices were quickly set to work shoveling the litter off the deck. They also climbed out onto the adjacent heaps and began scattering the tea widely over the open water, as if they were forking hay. Others jumped into the shallow water, cold as it was, to break up the shattered chests into smaller fragments and make certain that all had been emptied.

Hardly had the contents of the last chests been flung overboard than the tide turned, pushing the jettisoned tea back toward shore and eventually depositing it all along the harbor's rim from Griffin's Wharf to Dorchester Neck.

"The whole was done with very little tumult," Governor Hutchinson later conceded, and Joshua Wyeth declared that despite the fact that "we were merry, in an undertone, at the idea of making so large a cup of tea for the fishes," the "Indians" nevertheless "were as still as the nature of the case would admit, using no more words than were absolutely necessary.

"We stirred briskly in the business from the moment we left our dressing room," he wrote. "I never worked harder in my life.

"While we were unloading, the people crowded around us so as to be much in our way."

So sternly did participants and onlookers view the importance of destroying the tea, however, that only two minor attempts were made to snatch any of it.

One effort was made in a canoe, by a man described only as looking like "a countryman." John Hooton, eighteen, an oarmaker's apprentice

from the North End, saw the canoe gliding through the shadows alongside the ship on which he was working. He called an older man's attention to it, and was promptly ordered to "dislodge the interloper."
At once, "I and three or four other North Enders, as full of spirit as
myself, jumped over and beat the canoe from under him in the twin-
kling of an eye."

A more widely publicized attempt to make off with a private hoard
of free tea was reported briefly in the newspapers and described at
greater length by John Andrews. On December 18th he wrote:

> Not the least insult was offer'd to any person, save one Captain
> Conner, a letter of horses in this place, not many years remov'd
> from *dear Ireland*, who had ript up the lining of his coat and
> waistcoat under the arms, and watching his opportunity had
> nearly fill'd them with tea, but being detected, was handled pretty
> roughly. They not only stripp'd him of his cloaths but gave him
> a coat of mud, with a severe bruising into the bargain, and nothing
> but their utter aversion to make *any* disturbance prevented his
> being tar'd and feathered.

The young moon, which had not provided any appreciable radiance
for the goings-on, set at four minutes past eight o'clock.

III

When the Party was over, less than an hour later, all the disguised
militiamen were formed into ranks on the wharf and ordered to take
off their shoes and shake them until every vestige of clinging tea had
followed the contents of the smashed chests. Then, under command of
twenty-six-year-old Lendall Pitts, whose brother John was a member
of the Boston Board of Selectmen and whose father sat on the Governor's prestigious but recalcitrant Council, they marched off up Fort
Hill.

On the way, near the head of the wharf, the victorious troops passed
the house of a Tory named Coffin. Admiral Montagu happened to be
spending the night there, and as the column filed past, he pushed
open a window and called out, in his rough, blustering voice, "Well,
boys, you've had a fine, pleasant evening for your Indian caper, haven't
you? But mind, you've got to pay the fiddler yet!"

"Oh, never mind, Squire," Pitts mockingly yelled back. "Just come out here, if you please, and we'll settle the bill in two minutes."

Admiral Montagu slammed the window shut, and Pitts's men, with jeering laughter and exultant shouts, trudged on up the hill, stepping as briskly as they could to the puckish music of a fife.

Not all the tea was dumped at Griffin's Wharf, despite the elaborate precautions, but what survived was no threat to the market or to American resistance to the hated tax.

Thomas Melvill, twenty-two, late a divinity student at Princeton, by this time a fledgling Boston businessman, and eventually the grandfather of Herman Melville, found enough fragments in his shoes when he got home to fill a tiny bottle. The family kept it for years, and it is believed to be still in safekeeping.

Josiah Wheeler had worn boots that night, and when he took them off in front of his fireplace, a shower of tea descended upon the hearth. A woman neighbor, who had been keeping Mrs. Wheeler company while her husband was out on his escapade, exclaimed, "Oh, do save it! It'll make a nice mess."

Mrs. Wheeler wouldn't hear of it. She grabbed up her broom, said sharply, "Don't touch the cursed stuff!," and swept the tea leaves into the fire.

About ten o'clock Joseph Palmer and his friends James Foster Condy and Stephen Bruce, among the older participants in the raid, wearily reached Palmer's home. Mrs. Palmer, who had been nervously counting the hours in her parlor, heard the yard gate creak and then the front door squawk.

"I opened the parlor door," she later recalled, "and there stood three stout-looking Indians. I screamed, and should have fainted, but recognized my husband's voice saying, 'Don't be frightened, Betty. It is I. We have only been making a little salt-water tea.'"

Paying the Fiddler

(December 17, 1773—June 1, 1774)

I

IN a hasty note to Lord Dartmouth on the afternoon of December 17th, an indignant Governor Hutchinson wrote, "I sent expresses this morning before sunrise to summon a Council to meet me at Boston."

Hutchinson was writing under stringent time pressure. The brig *Dolphin*, which would bear his fateful message to the Secretary of State for the American Department, had been awaiting only a favoring wind before setting sail for London. The end of the previous day's rainstorm had brought that essential ingredient for a prompt departure. There was no telling how long the fair wind would hold.

Because of the urgent need to be brief, Hutchinson summarized the Boston Tea Party in one fairly short sentence. After quickly describing Rotch's mission to him, and the ship owner's dejected return with Hutchinson's negative reply to the mass meeting of December 16th, the Governor wrote, "Immediately thereupon numbers of the people cried out 'A Mob! a Mob!,' left the house, repaired to the wharf, where three of the vessels lay aground, having on board three hundred and forty chests of tea, and in two hours' time it was wholly destroyed." He added, "What influence this violence and outrage may have I cannot determine."

Three of his Council members had promptly pleaded indisposition, perhaps more of mind than body. In consequence, he lacked a quorum. Therefore, the Governor continued, "I have ordered new summons this afternoon, for the Council to meet me at Milton tomorrow morning."

He was not hopeful of the outcome. "Probably it may issue in a proclamation promising a reward for discovering the persons concerned, which has been the usual proceeding in other instances of high-handed riots."

Hutchinson concluded in haste: "The wind coming fair, I do not expect by this vessel to be able to give Your Lordship a more particular account of this unhappy affair."

Sam Adams was up and at work fully as early as the Governor that morning, scribbling terse accounts of the Tea Party to the Committees of Correspondence in Plymouth and Sandwich, and urging them to "behave with propriety and as becomes Men resolved to save their Country." He was determined to forestall, if possible, salvage of the tea aboard Captain Loring's wrecked *William* and its sequestering by the consignees (though, as we have seen, without success).

Adams also sent brief bulletins to the Committees of Correspondence of New York and Philadelphia, with which he had established important rapport during the previous year and a half. It was imperative now that they should know as soon as possible what Boston had done about its consignment of tea. Adams was as concise as Hutchinson in the telling of it:

> "The moment it was known out of doors that Mr. Rotch could not obtain a pass for his Ship by the Castle, a number of people huzza'd in the Street, and in a very little time every ounce of the Teas on board of the Captains Hall, Bruce & Coffin was immersed in the Bay, without the least injury to private property. The Spirit of the People on this occasion surprised all parties who view'd the Scene.
>
> We conceived it our duty to afford you the most early advice of this interesting event by express, which departing immediately obliges us to conclude.

The express was Paul Revere, who was galloping toward New York with Adams's messages before sun-up.

"Adams never was in greater glory," Governor Hutchinson commented with sarcasm in a prompt letter to Israel Mauduit in London, whom he felt he should inform of the outcome of the tea dispute as quickly as possible.

"Nobody suspected they [the townspeople] would suffer the tea to be destroyed," he declared, "there being so many men of property active at these meetings, as Hancock, Phillips, Rowe, Dennie, and others, besides the selectmen, and town clerk, who was clerk of all the meetings."

It was ironic that the Governor should have included John Rowe in his list. Rowe had attended only the meeting he was summoned to, had accepted a committee assignment only because he was afraid to turn it down, and had carefully remained at home during the day of the Tea Party and the day following.

By December 18th, Rowe ventured forth again, and was much distressed by what he heard and by his own consequent misgivings.

"The affair of Destroying the Tea makes Great Noise in the Town," he noted in his diary that day. "'Tis a Disastrous Affair & some People are much Alarmed. I can truly say I know nothing of the Matter nor who were concerned in it. I would rather have lost five hundred Guineas than Bruce should have taken any of this Tea on board his Ship."

The Boston *Gazette* assayed the town's mood and found it very different. At the conclusion of its quarter-column coverage of the Tea Party on Monday morning, December 20th, its first issue after the event, the *Gazette* stated, "The masters and owners are well pleas'd that their ships are thus clear'd; and the people are almost universally congratulating each other on this happy event."

Certainly many people were delighted.

"We are in perfect Jubilee," wrote a Whig from New York who was in town at the time. "The brave Bostonians . . . in spite of opposition and calumny, are an honor to mankind."

John Adams was in an exalted mood. Writing on December 17th to his old friend James Warren of Plymouth, he jubilantly declared:

> The die is cast. The people have passed the river and cut away the bridge. . . . This is the grandest event which has ever yet happened since the controversy with Britain opened. The sublimity of it charms me!
>
> For my part, I cannot express my own sentiments of it better than in the words of Colonel D. to me, last evening. . . . "The worst that can happen, I think," said he, "in consequence of it, will be that the province must pay for it. Now, I think the prov-

ince may pay for it, if it is drowned, as easily as if it is drunk;
and I think it is a matter of indifference whether it is drunk or
drowned. The province must pay for it in either case. But there
is this difference: I believe it will take them ten years to get the
province to pay for it; if so, we shall save ten years' interest of the
money, whereas, if it is drunk, it must be paid for immediately."
Thus he. However, he agreed with me that the province would
never pay for it; and also in this, that the final ruin of our constitution of government, and of all American liberties, would be
the certain consequence of suffering it to be landed.

Adams continued:

> Governor Hutchinson and his family and friends will never have
> done with their good services to Great Britain and the colonies.
> But for him, this tea might have been saved to the East India
> Company. Whereas this loss, if the rest of the colonies should fol-
> low our example, will, in the opinion of many persons, bankrupt
> the company. However, I dare say, the governor and consignees
> and custom-house officers in the other colonies will have more
> wisdom than ours have had, and take effectual care that their tea
> shall be sent back to England untouched; if not, it will as surely
> be destroyed there as it has been here.
>
> Threats, phantoms, bugbears, by the million, will be invented
> and propagated among the people upon this occasion. Individuals
> will be threatened with suits and prosecutions. Armies and navies
> will be talked of. Military executions, charters annulled, treason
> trials in England, and all that. But these terms are all but imagi-
> nations. Yet, if they should become realities, they had better be
> suffered than the great principle of parliamentary taxation be
> given up.
>
> The town of Boston never was more still and calm of a Saturday
> night than it was last night. All things were conducted with great
> order, decency, and *perfect submission to government*. No doubt
> we all thought the administration in better hands than it has been.

Governor Hutchinson's Council again lacked a quorum on December
18th. Its first full meeting was held at Cambridge on the 21st.

In his wrath and frustration immediately after the Tea Party, Governor Hutchinson at first told some individuals on the Council that
he was fully persuaded that the events of December 16th constituted

high treason. So wrote John Adams in a second letter to James Warren, dated December 22nd. The Governor had even "promised them the attendance of the attorney-general to prove it them out of law books." But the weakness of the case against the people of Boston and surrounding towns soon made itself embarrassingly clear. By December 21st, when the Council finally convened with Hutchinson at Cambridge, the Governor had backed down.

In discussing "the late proceedings," as Adams called them, Hutchinson now had retreated enough so that he was "rather of the opinion they were burglary. I suppose he meant what we call New England burglary, that is, breaking open a shop or ship, &c., which is punished with branding, &c.

"But the Council thought it would look rather awkward," Adams went on, "to issue a proclamation against the whole community, and therefore contented themselves with ordering Mr. Attorney to prosecute such as he should know or be informed of."

This would lead nowhere, as Hutchinson knew only too well. Indeed, as he described the situation later in his *History of Massachusetts Bay,* "there was not a justice of peace, sheriff, constable, or peace officer in the province who would venture to take cognizance of any breach of law against the general bent of the people." Moreover, "so many of the actors and abetters were universally known that a proclamation with a reward for discovery would have been ridiculed. The attorney-general, therefore, was ordered to lay the matter before the grand jury, who there was no room to expect would ever find a bill for what they did not consider as an offence."

The only punitive action taken in Boston as an immediate consequence of the Tea Party was the arrest of a barber named Eckley, who had evidently yielded to an occupational tendency to talk too much. A neighbor of his tattled to the authorities. Eckley had indeed taken part in the raid on the tea ships, but he no sooner landed in jail than the sheriff was anonymously threatened with tarring and feathering. There was no testimony against Eckley that would stand up in court, and the sheriff soon released him. The neighbor who was responsible for Eckley's brief fright and inconvenience was, however, liberally coated with tar and feathers and borne naked through the cold streets on a narrow pole with a placard reading "Informer" slung around his neck.

Balked by his Council, Governor Hutchinson was still seething with rage when he wrote to Isaac Williams of Hatfield on December 23rd.

> There never was greater tyranny in Constantinople than has
> been lately in Boston. Because a number of gentlemen who, with-
> out their knowledge, the East India Company made the consignees
> of 400 chests of Tea would not send it back again, which was
> absolutely out of their power, they have forced them to fly to the
> Castle for refuge and then have destroyed the property committed
> to their care. Such barbarity none of the Aborigines were ever
> guilty of. The Admiral asked some of them next morning who was
> to pay the fidler. . . .

Paul Revere rode back into Boston two days after Christmas, "per-
forming his Journey in a much shorter Time than could be expected
at this Season of the year." He brought heartening word that, when
news of the Tea Party reached New York and Philadelphia, church
bells were rung and citizens in crowded coffee houses wildly cheered
the courage and achievement of their brethren in Boston.

New York's Whigs had been on the verge of accepting a compromise
with the Governor and consignees that would have allowed the tea,
when it reached there, to be stored in the army barracks until it could
be returned to London. Instead, inspired by Boston's boldness, they
now insisted that when the tea ship appeared, its captain should be
told to return to London immediately, anchoring off Sandy Hook only
long enough to reprovision. It should not be allowed to enter the harbor.

[Actually, *Nancy*, the tea ship bound for New York, had been blown
so far off course in the autumnal gales that she had finally landed at
Antigua, in the British West Indies, and had to be refitted. When the
vessel at last found its roundabout way to Sandy Hook the following
April, the captain was handed Governor Tryon's order to turn around
and go back to Britain. He promptly obeyed.

Philadelphia's tea ship, *Polly*, bringing one of that city's consignees,
Gilbert Barclay, as a passenger, arrived off Chester in the Delaware
River on Christmas Day. There it was hailed by a committee of citizens
from Philadelphia, who persuaded Barclay to resign his commission
and Captain Ayres to take *Polly* back to London. The river pilots had
already vowed not to guide *Polly* upstream to Philadelphia anyway, so
Captain Ayres's decision was prudent. By January 27th, he was sailing

safely up the Thames instead, Barclay making the voyage with him.

Charleston's tea had arrived there on December 2nd. There were many wordy meetings of merchants and planters in regard to it, but the men could not reach a satisfactory decision. The consignees, however, felt sufficiently cowed to refuse to accept the cargo. At the end of twenty days, it was unloaded without hindrance and stored in a damp warehouse. There it eventually rotted.]

Boston alone had defied the King's government in militant fashion, broken the law, and destroyed its tea in unflinching demonstration of its convictions, merely professed in the chief towns of the other provinces. By so doing, it won widespread admiration and backing there that might have been lacking otherwise. When Parliament reacted with punitive legislation aimed at Boston, it unified the provinces as never before.

Many men in Boston were anxious to tell their side of the story of the Boston Tea Party to friends and sympathizers in London as soon as possible. As we have seen, Governor Hutchinson wrote his own version for Lord Dartmouth the following day, though the fickleness of the wind prevented its leaving Boston aboard *Dolphin* until December 23rd.

On that same day, Captain Scott sailed Hancock's *Hayley* out of the harbor on its first London voyage since it brought Jonathan Clarke home. With him he carried Dr. Hugh Williamson of Philadelphia as a passenger. Dr. Williamson not only had watched the Tea Party in progress but took with him personal letters to Arthur Lee, diplomatic agent in London for the Province of Massachusetts, from Samuel Adams, Dr. Joseph Warren, and John Scollay—Scollay's letter being the one containing his opinion of how the crisis could have been avoided (as we have seen in a previous section).

Adams, confident of Lee's entire sympathy with those who had staged the Tea Party, wrote that "you cannot imagine the height of joy that sparkles in the eyes and animates the countenance as well as the hearts of all we meet on this occasion, excepting the disappointed, disconcerted Hutchinson and his tools. . . . He (the governor) is now, I am told, consulting his lawyers and books to make out that the resolves of the meeting [of December 16th] are treasonable. . . ."

Dr. Warren wrote, in part, "I fear that unless a speedy alteration is made in the system of American policy, a few years will render us as indifferent to the interests of the mother-country as to that of any other State in Europe. . . .

"This country," he said, "is inhabited by a people loyal to their king and faithful to themselves; none will more cheerfully venture their lives and fortunes for the honor and defence of the prince who reigns in their hearts, and none will with more resolution oppose the tyrant who dares to invade their rights."

Dr. Warren stressed the formidable American opposition to tea that bore a tax.

"It is certain," he assured Lee, "the whole navy of Britain will not prevent the introduction of Dutch tea, nor will her armies prevail with us to use the English tea while the act imposing a duty on that article remains unrepealed."

In Governor Hutchinson's view, tyranny had nothing to do with the recalcitrance of his exasperating fellow-countrymen. Tyranny, he said, didn't exist in America.

"The prevalence of a spirit of opposition to government in the plantation is the natural consequence of the great growth of Colonies so remote from the parent State," he declared in a thoughtful letter to William Robertson, the Scottish historian, on December 28th, "not the effect of oppression in the King or his servants, as the promoters of this spirit would have the world to believe."

Hutchinson had no uneasy second thoughts about the righteousness of his own course during the anxious days that led to the Tea Party.

On January 1st, in a letter to Sir Francis Bernard, a previous Royal Governor of Massachusetts, Hutchinson wrote:

> The destruction of the tea is an unfortunate event, and it was what everybody supposed impossible, after so many men of property had made part of the meetings and were in danger of being liable for the value of it.
>
> It would have given me a much more painful reflection if I had saved it by any concession to a lawless and highly criminal assembly of men, to whose proceedings the loss must be consequently attributed, and the probability is that it was a part of their plan from the beginning.

Three days later, he assured Samuel Swift:

> I think you will be satisfied of the propriety of my conduct in the particular instance you refer to, when I put you in mind that

I have taken a solemn oath, as Governor, to do every thing in my power that the acts of trade may be carried into execution.

Now, to have granted a pass to a vessel which I knew had not cleared at the custom-house would have been such a direct countenancing and encouraging the violation of the acts of trade that I believe you would have altered your opinion of me, and seen me ever after in an unfavorable light.

"I am sure, if I could have preserved the property that is destroyed, or could have complied with the general¯desire of the people, consistent with the duty which my station requires, I would most readily have done it."

It is a wonder that the letters sent to Arthur Lee at Christmastime by Adams, Warren, and Scollay did not go to the bottom of the Atlantic. *Hayley*, which carried them all to London, endured one of its worst voyages. Dr. Williamson probably never forgot it. Though the vessel reached the relatively calm and safe waters of the Downs, off the Kentish coast in the Strait of Dover, within twenty-eight days after leaving Boston, its passage had been a nightmare.

Writing to John Hancock from London when it was all over, Captain Scott reported:

I had some very Bad Weather on the Passage and a few days after I left you all the Tarr between decks Under the Cables got Loose and there was no Chance of securing them for the weather Continuing bad we had no opportunity to open the Hatches till the 4 of January to haul the cables upon deck, When I found many of the Casks got Bung down and run entirely Out and several stove [so] that the Deck was all over in such a Condition that what Casks remaned full we could not possibly Secure and I was Oblig'd to throw over Board full and Empty 73 Barrels and afterwards took up not less than a dozen Barrells of Tarr off the Deck. If the ship had happened to have been leaky It would have been very bad for us for the pump Well got full of Tarr and the pumps would not work.

Lord Frederick North, prime minister of Great Britain at the time of the Boston Tea Party, looked so much like King George III that their fathers joked about it.

II

On the morning after the Tea Party, Lord Dartmouth happened to send a request to Edward Wheler, vice-chairman of the East India Company, to drop in at his office in Whitehall to discuss "some advices Lord Dartmouth has lately received from America respecting the importation of tea from England."

The advices were at least a month and a half old, but when the two men met, on Monday, December 20th, they soon decided that the contents of the dispatches were sufficiently disturbing to justify the East India Company's making an immediate round-robin appeal to the London representatives of all American tea consignees to send in the most recent letters they had received from the colonies regarding the tea.

The results of this canvass were far more upsetting. Though the latest communications had been sent off early in November, they contained ominous news. The last letter from Faneuil and Winslow in Boston, dated November 4th, gave an account of the attack on the Clarkes' warehouse. From New York had come word, dated November 5th, that "the introduction of the East India Company's tea is violently opposed here, by a set of men who shamefully live by monopolizing tea in the smuggling way."

Lord Dartmouth and the East India Company directors could do little more than worry, however. Parliament was enjoying its long recess, which had begun the previous August and would last beyond mid-January. Even then, many members anticipated that "we are to have no material business before us" in the coming session. Many government officials were away from London. Dartmouth himself had been on prolonged vacation and would be leaving town again for the extensive Christmas holidays.

When, eventually, Lord Dartmouth would receive the news of the Tea Party, he could not be depended on to defend the colonials before an outraged Parliament. "Lord Dartmouth is truly a good man," Benjamin Franklin had written to his son a few months earlier, "and wishes sincerely a good understanding with the colonies, but does not seem to have the strength equal to his wishes."

In particular, Dartmouth was easily swayed by his step-brother, Lord North, who in turn was always ready to jump at the King's bidding. In the last analysis, it was the King's reaction that was to be feared. Here again was a basically good man, but a stubborn and not very bright

King George III, in a portrait miniature done when he was about thirty-five years old, his age at the time of the events chronicled in this book.

one. "He has in some cases a great share of what his friends call *firm-ness*," Franklin confided wryly to his son. It has been said that the King mistook stubbornness for courage.

During the first half of January, 1774, Lord Dartmouth received a scattering of letters from Boston, New York, Philadelphia, and Charleston, forwarded to him by the East India Company. They must have made him increasingly apprehensive, for they accurately reflected the rising resentment against the expected tea ships and their cargoes.

It was not until January 19th, when *Hayley* reached Dover, that the American Secretary learned of what had happened in Boston on the night of December 16th. The news had evidently been sent to London by courier from Falmouth, where the vessel first put in.

The King learned about it at once, and before he went to bed that night he wrote a note to Lord Dartmouth, beginning "I am much hurt that the instigation of bad men hath again drawn the people of Boston to take such unjustifiable steps." The King's hurt soon turned to anger.

All London had the news three days later, when the first newspaper account, reproducing the Boston *Gazette*'s story of December 20th, was published.

By January 27th, Dartmouth had Hutchinson's note of December 17th in hand. He also had had a chance to read an anonymous letter sent from Boston on the same day to George Dudley, one of the East India Company's Board of Governors, by someone who signed himself "Anglo Americanus." This letter, baldly beginning "Your tea is destroyed," made the mood of the colonies unmistakable. Declaring that "the people were obliged to destroy it . . . or else, by an unlawful unrighteous Act imposing a duty, this tea would have destroyed them." Then the letter continued:

> There is the utmost detestation of tea. Even some of our country towns have collected all the tea they had by them and burnt it in their public common, as so much chains and slavery. Get the Tea Act repealed and you'll sell all your tea. Otherwise you must keep all. The people will risk life and fortune in this affair—the very being of America depends on it.
>
> I am sorry the Company are led into such a scrape by the Ministry, to try the Americans' bravery at the expense of their property. The artifice of the Ministry is to dispose of your tea and preserve

the vile Tea Act, but they'll miss their aim—the Americans will not swallow cheap tea which has a poison in the heart of it. They see the hook through the bait. I am a well-wisher to the Company, and also to America, but death to an American is more desirable than slavery.

Britain's reaction, on the other hand, was strong, very widespread anger and resentment. Parliament returned to London determined to teach the Americans a lesson. "The town of Boston must be knocked down about their ears and destroyed," one Member raged.

[On the heels of this sober news came the silly rumor to the effect that some people in Boston were complaining that the fish they caught tasted very odd, and it was suggested that the hundreds of chests of tea thrown overboard "may have so contaminated the water in the harbour that the fish may have contracted a disorder not unlike the nervous complaints of the human body." One Boston correspondent even imagined that the Newfoundland fisheries might in time be affected.]

Parliament's mood was not improved by the arrival in the Thames on Thursday, January 25th, of the ship *Polly*, sluggishly moving upstream with all the tea the Philadelphians had rejected.

There was a Cabinet meeting at night on January 29th, attended by the full roster of seven ministers. Only Lords North and Dartmouth, among them, were inclined to moderation. These gentlemen agreed to provide Parliament with all papers relating to the colonial troubles, as the Earl of Buckinghamshire had already proposed in the House of Lords. More importantly, the Cabinet resolved "that in consequence of the present disorders in America, effectual steps be taken to secure the Dependence of the Colonies on the Mother Country." That was to be the primary goal of the various punitive measures that Parliament would devise in the course of the following few months.

III

In Boston, meanwhile, the catharsis of destroying the tea having been achieved, the population was going about its normal business as best it could in a winter that, after a deceptively mild start, had turned severe.

Not all the spirit of December 16th had fled, though, for on New Year's Eve there were minor manifestations of it in both Charlestown and Boston. John Rowe's diary entry for December 31st read:

> The People of Charlestown collected what Tea they could find in The Town & burnt it in the View of a thousand spectators. There was found in the House of One Withington of Dorchester about half a Chest of Tea—the People gathered together & took the Tea, Brought it into the Common of Boston & Burnt it this night about eleven of Clock. This is supposed to be part of the Tea that was taken out of the Ships & floated over to Dorchester.

At least one tentative individual effort was soon made to bridge the chasm that had suddenly opened up in British-American relations.

John Rowe decided to talk matters over with his former crony Admiral Montagu, who had notified him after the Tea Party that he would no longer be buying naval supplies from Rowe. The friendly gesture was rebuffed.

"I paid Admiral Montague a visit this morning & found him very Angry, I think without reason," Rowe wrote as his diary entry for January 7th. "Be that as it may, if he is Angry he may be pleased again &c. I wish the Good Wishes of All Mankind & should Esteem his Favour, but as for his Business—that dont give me any Concern. He has taken it away without Just Cause."

A tendency to wonder if the destroyed tea oughtn't to be paid for was beginning to make itself evident elsewhere in the colonies, if not yet in Boston. General Sir Frederick Haldimand, acting commander-in-chief of His Majesty's armed forces in North America during the temporary absence of General Gage, wrote Lord Dartmouth from New York on January 5th that there was widespread disapproval in that province—perhaps in Tory circles only—of Boston's drastic action and a feeling that the town ought to be made to pay for its impulsive disposition of the tea.

A move in Boston to raise money by subscription to compensate the East India Company for the town's "late frantic behaviour" was reported to Dartmouth three weeks later.

Even Benjamin Franklin, writing from London to Thomas Cushing on February 2nd, suggested that paying for the tea destroyed would be the quickest way of calming down the British government and achieving some kind of compromise. Legislatures more than once had compensated private citizens for the destruction of property by unknown persons, he pointed out. After all, Franklin said, the East India Company was not America's enemy.

Franklin's suggestion infuriated Samuel Adams, who sniffily disapproved of Franklin's amoral life style and had never liked him anyway. "He may be a great philosopher, but he's a bungling politician," Adams remarked scornfully.

Adams, naturally, would exonerate the people altogether from responsibility for the Tea Party. "In short the Governor," he said to Arthur Lee in a letter dated January 25th, "who for Art & Cunning as well as an inveterate hatred of the people was inferior to no one of the Cabal, both encouraged & provoked the people to destroy the Tea. . . . In this View of the Matter the Question is easily decided who ought in Justice to pay for the Tea if it ought to be paid for at all."

Governor Hutchinson's efforts to find culprits on whom responsibility for the Tea Party could be pinned with some chance of its sticking had proved fruitless, as he had glumly anticipated. The participants were remarkably solid in keeping silent. Doubtless Joshua Wyeth expressed their common feeling when he wrote, "We pretended to be as zealous to find out the perpetrators as the rest, and were all so close and loyal that the whole affair remained in Egyptian darkness."

Most Bostonians at this time were only too glad to stay indoors and keep to themselves, for January was a very cold month, according to Deacon John Tudor's diary. By the end of it, he wrote, there was "fine sledding for 200 miles to the Westward as Travelers tell us and Snow in general 3 feet deep."

Out at Castle William, on January 9th, Thomas Hutchinson, Jr., reported to his brother Elisha, who by this time had stealthily made his way home to Middleborough, that he himself "stole up" to Milton for a brief visit but had returned to the island. He had one bit of cheering news: "The tea saved out of Loring is housed at the Castle." (Jonathan Clarke's secret foray to the Cape had resulted in the shifting of 58 chests of tea from Captain Loring's disintegrating brig *William* to a lighter, which brought it safely to Castle William on December 30th.)

[As could be expected Samuel Adams was indignant at the success of this coup.

"It is said that the Indians this way, if they had suspected the Marshpee Tribe [early inhabitants of Cape Cod] would have been so sick at the knees, would have march'd on snow shoes . . . to have done the Business for them," he wrote disgustedly to James Warren of Plymouth on January 10th. "However, it may all be for the best, for while the Tea remains at the Castle it may hang (as Edes & Gill express it) like a Millstone about the Necks of the Consignees."]

"The Bostonians now say we shall not return to town without making concessions," Tom Hutchinson's January 9th letter to Elisha continued. "For my own part I shall not be in a hurry, nor much grieved, if I do not see it this twelvemonths, but I suppose shall quit the Castle some time this week, as we all are provided with retreats in the country. I have had a disagreeable six weeks of it, but am in hopes the issue will be well."

On that same day, Francis Rotch, having lodged a legal protest against all the consignees for "damages we have sustained by the said tea being kept in our ship by your not giving the necessary orders or directions about it"—damages that he somewhat apologetically assessed at slightly more than £289—but nevertheless having signed himself their "assured friend," boarded his ship *Dartmouth* and sailed for London to find out where he stood with the East India Company and the government.

Tom Hutchinson's blithe expectations of escaping from the Castle soon were realized, but he merely exchanged one place of exile for another. He and Benjamin Faneuil one day left the Castle together, but word of their departure quickly reached Boston. Handbills from the Loyal Nine were posted, threatening them with tarring and feathering if they showed up in town. Faneuil's nerve failed, and he retreated to the safety of the fort. Young Hutchinson succeeded in reaching Milton, where he wrote to Elisha on January 21st:

> Mr. Faneuil is since returned to the Castle, and I am really more confined than if I was there, as I keep pretty close to my room.
> Mr. Jonathan Clarke sails in a few days for England, in a ship, Coffin, Master, of which I am very glad, as it may prevent misrepresentations of our conduct on that side the water.

Clarke managed to depart for London in Captain Coffin's *Beaver* before the end of the month.

Elisha Hutchinson had in the meantime made the careless mistake of taking his wife to visit her father, Colonel Watson, in Plymouth.

The local Committee of Correspondence soon discovered that the Hutchinsons were there, and roused a hostile crowd against them, so threatening that they felt obliged to flee town in a blizzard.

His brother Tom, writing from Milton on February 4th, had learned of this and remarked, "I wish you had not gone to Plymouth at all, but what has hap'ned cou'd not have been foreseen.

"If we are able to live quiet in our retreats," Tom went on, "it is as much as I expect at present, as I am sure no opposition will avail anything. Perhaps the Honorable Judges of the Superior Court may screen the poor Consignees, as I am told the flame is kindling fast against them, & it is thought it will not be safe for them to come to Court unless they comply with every demand made of them; their stations will not be the least security to them.

"The Governor seems determined to go to England," Tom added, "unless prevented by the Lieutenant Governor's declining state, which I think increases upon him very fast.

"What do you think of giving up the Store? I am told it is kept shut up, & the few things in it may easily be removed."

Ann Hulton, assuming that all the consignees were still at the Castle, thought they were lost men. Writing on January 31st to her old friend Mrs. Lightbody in Liverpool, she declared that "there is no prospect of their ever returning & residing in Boston with Safety. This place & all the Towns about entered into a written agreement not to afford them any Shelter or protection, so that they are not only banished from their families & homes, but their retreat is cut off, & their interest greatly injured by ruining their Trade."

Further, the consignees shortly lost an important friend. Lieutenant-Governor Andrew Oliver, whose health had rapidly been failing for several months, died on March 3rd, at the age of sixty-eight. Governor Hutchinson had long before asked Lord Dartmouth for six months' leave to come to England, and been granted it, but now he was obliged to stick to his post until relieved. It was an agonizing necessity.

At Oliver's formal funeral, held on March 8th, the Governor's Company of Cadets was present in full regalia, with Colonel John Hancock at their head. When friends of Hancock's deplored his willingness to attend the rite, he said he was simply showing proper respect for the office, not the man. But when Oliver's coffin was lowered into the icy ground, riffraff on the outskirts of the gathering broke into raucous cheers, to the shock and disgust of assembled Whigs and Tories alike.

IV

By mid-February, a dozen Americans had reached London who could give first-hand accounts to government officials of the events leading up to the Tea Party and the details of that "very riotous proceeding," as Horace Walpole called it. They included Dr. Hugh Williamson, Francis Rotch, Captain James Hall of *Dartmouth*, Captain James Scott of *Hayley*, and others. Lord Dartmouth summoned them all to a meeting of the Privy Council on the evening of February 19th.

The witnesses spoke freely, but were too vague about the identity of the participants to enable Attorney General Thurlow and Solicitor General Wedderburn to proceed with their initially announced intention of bringing charges of high treason against individuals involved.

These legal gentlemen had, indeed, drawn up a list of prime suspects. It included William Molineux, Dr. Joseph Warren, Jonathan Williams, Samuel Adams, Doctor Thomas Young, and, of all people, Doctor Benjamin Church, who was in the pay of General Gage. Thurlow and Wedderburn had hoped to have these persons arrested and brought to England for trial.

Nine days later, after reviewing the testimony given before the Privy Council on February 19th, and reading newspaper reports and correspondence from Boston, the Attorney General and Solicitor General were embarrassingly obliged to agree that there was not sufficient evidence to sustain charges of treason against any of the men on their list of suspects.

The King was annoyed and disappointed, and Parliament, which had had all the trouble from Boston it could stomach, moved grimly ahead with legislation that would punish the innocent along with the guilty.

The Earl of Buckinghamshire had told the House of Lords a month before, "The question now is not about the liberty of North America but whether we are to be free or slaves to our colonies." And the House of Commons underscored its determination to demonstrate who was in charge by drawing up a series of so-called Coercive Acts.

The King had set the tone of their actions in his message to Parliament on March 7th, which Lord North had read to Commons. Speaking of the Americans, and especially the Bostonians, the King had written, "We must master them or totally leave them to themselves and treat them as aliens."

A political cartoon, attributed to Paul Revere, showing Lord North trying to force tea down Boston's throat while Chief Justice Peter Oliver holds her arms and his brother, the Lieutenant Governor, holds her feet. At left, Governor Hutchinson and King George III link arms conspiratorily.

George III had expressed himself even more intemperately at a recent levee. There, reported Horace Walpole, he had shocked his listeners by saying, "I'd as lief fight the Bostonians as the French." More shocking still, Walpole commented, was the fact that the King had laughed when he said it.

First among Parliament's punitive measures came the Boston Port Bill. Lord North read the text to Commons on March 14th. Here was its essence: Boston Harbor was to be closed to all foreign shipping beginning June 1st. No vessels from abroad could enter after that date; none that were in port would be allowed to leave after June 15th. The customhouse was to be moved to Salem. Only coastal lighters, carefully inspected first, would be permitted to bring fuel and essential supplies to the people of Boston.

"This punishment is intended to continue," Lord North explained, "until indemnities have been paid to the East India Company for the destruction of its tea, until the injured royal officers have been compensated, and until the King judges that peace is so restored that trade can continue."

There was, indeed, almost no opposition. Even America's best friends in Parliament were inclined to approve, including the usually dependable Colonel Barré, who now said he thought Boston deserved punishment.

There was somewhat wider protest against it in the House of Lords, but the Bill was passed overwhelmingly on March 30th.

Benjamin Franklin tried to warn his compatriots of what was in store for them. Writing from London to Thomas Cushing on March 22nd, he said, "The violent destruction of the tea seems to have united all parties here against our province, so that the bill now brought into Parliament for shutting up Boston as a port till satisfaction is made, meets with no opposition."

The next move was to amend the charter of Massachusetts: (1) Beginning August 1st, the Governor's Council was no longer to be elected by the General Court but named by the King; (2) the Governor was to be allowed to appoint and remove all judges and officers of the law; (3) there were to be no more town meetings unless the King permitted them; and (4) freeholders were no longer to be permitted to select juries after September 1st.

Introduction of this second Coercive Act brought a scathing comment from William Dowdeswell in Commons. He declared, "You are not now contending for a point of honour, you are struggling to obtain a most ridiculous superiority."

Parliament was unmoved by such reproofs. It passed the Regulating Bill, as it was called, by a lopsided majority on May 11th.

Almost simultaneously, more debates were in progress on a third coercive measure, a Bill for the Impartial Administration of Justice. In essence, this measure proposed to enable the Royal Governor of Massachusetts to shift trials to another province or to England whenever he felt true impartiality was impossible at home. The true purpose, which every member of Parliament could recognize, was to protect colonial administrators from local revenge by process of law and to shield soldiers from hostile colonial juries in case they were obliged to get rough in enforcing the Coercive Acts or any other laws. This was, in effect, substituting martial law for civil law.

Even Governor Hutchinson, who had been criticized in certain quarters for not having called out the military to forestall the Boston Tea Party, disapproved of this kind of administration. Without knowing, of course, that the Justice Bill was forthcoming, he remarked to Lord Dartmouth in a letter written March 22nd that "I have not been satisfied that there have yet been any such rebellious insurrections as would have justified the representative of the King in bringing forward the military power in order to suppress them." And when Hutchinson got to England, in July, he told Solicitor General Wedderburn the same thing.

The Justice Bill (which soon became its common name) roused the most spirited opposition of all. Colonel Barré, by now thoroughly repelled by the minatory mood of Parliament, delivered a magnificent speech against the measure on April 15th. Its final paragraphs well deserve recalling, beginning with a pertinent query to the House:

> Who is to execute it? He must be a bold man indeed who makes the attempt. If the people are so exasperated that it is unsafe to bring the man who has injured them to trial, let the governor who withdraws him from justice look to himself. The people will not endure it; they would no longer deserve the reputation of being descended from the loins of Englishmen if they did endure it.
>
> When I stand up as an advocate for America, I feel myself the firmest friend of *this* country. We stand upon the commerce of America. Alienate your colonies, and you will subvert the founda-

tion of your riches and your strength. Let the banners of rebellion be once spread in America, and you are an undone people. You are urging this desperate, this destructive issue. You are urging it with such violence, and by measure tending so manifestly to that fatal point, that, but that a state of madness only could inspire such an intention, it would appear to be your deliberate purpose.

In assenting to your late bill [the Boston Port Act], I resisted the violence of America at the hazard of my popularity there. I now resist your frenzy at the same risk here. You have changed your ground. You are becoming the aggressors, and offering the last of human outrages to the people of America, by subjecting them, in effect, to military execution.

I know the vast superiority of your disciplined troops over the provincials, but beware how you supply the want of discipline by desperation. Instead of sending them the olive branch, you have sent the naked sword. By the olive branch I mean a repeal of all the late laws, fruitless to you, and oppressive to them."

And then the earnest Colonel concluded:

Ask their aid in a constitutional manner, and they will give it to the utmost of their ability. They never yet refused it when properly required. Your journals bear the recorded acknowledgments of the zeal with which they have contributed to the general necessities of the state.

What madness is it that prompts you to attempt obtaining that by force which you may more certainly procure by requisition?

They may be flattered into anything, but they are too much like yourselves to be driven. Have some indulgence for your own likeness. Respect their sturdy English virtue. Retract your odious exertions of authority, and remember that the first step towards making them contribute to your wants is to reconcile them to your government."

All that splendid, sincere eloquence was wasted. The Justice Bill, so incongruously named, passed easily on May 18th. The King gave his consent to both it and the Regulating Bill two days later.

Parliament also rushed through a fourth measure to bring the American colonists to heel. For years the law had permitted the quartering of British troops in uninhabited houses and inns in the provinces. This new bill provided for their billeting with private families whenever that was required—as in instances of civil disturbances within towns, though that possibility was not mentioned.

There had been so many disputes over the earlier law that it was obvious that the new one would be almost impossible to enforce. Nevertheless, it was whisked through Parliament, passed in late May, and was on its way to General Gage, at Boston, by June 3rd.

General Gage, ordered to return to his post as commander-in-chief of the North American forces and also authorized to relieve Thomas Hutchinson as Governor for the six months' vacation he had requested, had sailed for Boston on the warship *Lively* on April 18th. With him had sailed troop replacements and reinforcements.

V

Ignorant of what was impending, Boston had spent a largely tranquil winter.

There had been a flare-up of the bravado of December 16th when fifty members of the "Narragansett Tribe" swarmed over Captain Benjamin Gorham's ship *Fortune* upon its arrival in Boston from London on March 7th, found twenty-eight chests of tea on board, "and emptied every Chest of that pernicious and Obnoxious herb in the Ocean."

For the most part, though, there had been so little stir or controversy to ruffle the town's calm that John Adams on April 9th began his diary entry with "Still! silent as midnight! The first vessels may bring us tidings which will erect the crests of the Tories again, and depress the spirits of the Whigs," but meanwhile all was dismally dull. Adams had begun to feel that the issue might not be settled during his lifetime.

"There is not spirit enough on either side to bring the question to a complete decision," he wrote.

All this changed on May 10th. On that Monday morning, the Boston *Gazette* first printed the full text of the Port Bill.

The town was aghast, but indignation quickly overcame dismay. First evidence of its temper came at the polls, for May 10th was a town election day. Hancock, Sam Adams, Cushing, and Phillips were up for reelection. Hancock won every vote. Adams missed unanimous endorsement by only one vote. The other candidates garnered very heavy pluralities.

Next move was to convoke the Committees of Correspondence of

Boston and seven other towns on May 12th. They condemned the Port Bill as unjust and cruel, and scorned the suggestion that they might escape this harsh penalty by paying for the tea.

On the same day, Samuel Adams dispatched a circular letter to the other provinces. "This attack," he wrote in his best declamatory style, "though made immediately upon us, is doubtless designed for every other colony who shall not surrender their sacred rights and liberties into the hands of an infamous ministry. Now, therefore, is the time when *all* should be united in opposition to this violation of the liberties of all."

Adams called upon the other provinces, if they should agree with him that Boston was now "suffering in the common cause," to cease all trade with Great Britain at once. "If this should be done, you will please consider it will be through a voluntary suffering greatly short of what we are called to endure from the immediate hand of tyranny."

A town meeting was then called for May 13th. Sam Adams was chosen moderator. There was a strong move by the Tories present to have the voters agree to pay for the tea, but it was buried under an avalanche of "Nays." The Whigs declared that such a move would be an admission that they had been wrong and the principle for which they had been fighting so stubbornly was invalid.

Adams was buoyantly confident that the other provinces and towns would rally to Boston's support, as they did. Summarizing the town meeting's vote in another circular letter, he wrote:

> The people receive the edict with indignation. It is expected by their enemies, and feared by some of their friends, that this town singly will not be able to support the cause under so severe a trial. As the very being of every colony, considered as a free people, depends upon the event, a thought so dishonorable to our brethren cannot be entertained as that this town will be left to struggle alone.

By the whim of wind and wave, which produced exceedingly bad timing, the *Lively* brought General Gage into Boston Harbor while the town meeting of May 13th was in progress. With the General came four regiments of troops, replacing those that had been stationed at Castle William and increasing substantially the number of British soldiers assigned to Boston. They stopped over for four days at Castle William, but on May 17th the new Royal Governor of Massachusetts, who was to conduct provincial affairs while Thomas Hutchinson was away, entered the town in style.

Colonel Hancock and his Cadets were there to provide an honor guard, somewhat wilted in splendor by a chilly rain. British officers, American Whigs and Tories, sat down together to a banquet in Faneuil Hall, at which they managed to preserve courtesy and the appearance of friendliness. But, outside, the new British troops were already putting up their tents on Boston Common, and the true mood of the town was dark indeed.

"Imagine to yourself the horror painted in the faces of a string of slaves condemn'd by the Inquisition to perpetual drudgery at the oar!" exclaimed John Andrews next day in a letter to his friend in Philadelphia. "Such is the dejection imprinted on every countenance we meet in this once happy, but now totally ruin'd town. . . . Nothing will save us but an entire stoppage of trade, both to England and the West Indies, throughout the continent; and that must be determin'd as speedily as absolutely."

On the sunny morning of June 1st, a day of beguiling charm and freshness, Thomas Hutchinson left his cherished hilltop home in Milton, said goodbye to his neighbors, and made his way to the harbor, where he was rowed out to the warship *Minerva*. Lord Dartmouth had written that he and the King fully approved Hutchinson's stand in the recent troubles, that the King was waiting to give him an appropriate mark of his esteem. (Hutchinson was later offered a baronetcy, but declined it.) A large number of friends and associates had signed a testimonial of their affection and respect for him, and their thanks for all he had done for his native Massachusetts during a lifetime of public service there.

All this was comforting, but Hutchinson could not throw off his mood of deep depression. Appropriately, though not because of his departure, the church bells of Boston were tolling; many of the townspeople wore mourning. This was the day the Port Bill, which Hutchinson thought far too stringent, took effect.

Hutchinson could not have known then that he would never return, but he may have sensed that he was beginning exile, that he would spend the rest of his days in England longing to go home to the land he loved.

A few months earlier, an Englishman signing himself "Raleigh" had written an open letter to Lord Dartmouth, foretelling the outcome of the policy being implemented that day in Boston. The letter, published in *Gentlemen's Magazine*, concluded with the prescient warning:

"My Lord, an attempt to establish government in America by military force must be ultimately fatal to this country. It will commence in folly and injustice—it will end in distress and humiliation."

And so it did.

Appendix

Chronology of Events, 1773-74

1773

February—To avoid bankruptcy, East India Company petitions Parliament for huge loan and permission to market surplus tea, duty free, in American colonies.

May 10—Parliament passes Tea Act, granting East India Company exemption from domestic tea duties but retaining hated import tax of three pence per pound on all tea sold to Americans.

June-July—London representatives of various leading American tea merchants petition East India Company to choose their clients as consignees. Jonathan Clarke of Boston, in London to buy tea for family firm, Richard Clarke & Sons, conducts own campaign for favor.

August 4—East India Company announces selection of tea consignees. Chosen for Boston: Thomas Hutchinson, Jr., and brother Elisha, sons of Royal Governor of Massachusetts; Benjamin Faneuil, Jr.; Joshua Winslow; and Richard Clarke & Sons.

August-October—Various tea ships selected in London, loaded, and dispatched in turn to American ports. For Boston: ships *Dartmouth* and *Eleanor*, brigs *Beaver* and *William*.

October 18—Weekly Boston *Gazette* publishes first firm news of Tea Act and names of local men rumored to be consignees; roundly condemns both Act and abettors.

October 25—Boston *Gazette* steps up attacks on Tea Act and consignees. Virulent campaign continues through following weeks.

November 2—Anonymous summonses delivered after midnight to doors of tea consignees demand public resignation of roles next day under Liberty Tree at noon.

November 3 (morning)—Angry tea consignees and defiant friends meet at Richard Clarke's warehouse and agree to ignore summonses.

November 3 (afternoon)—Crowd irked at non-appearance of consignees at Liberty Tree moves to Clarke warehouse and attempts to attack occupants.

November 4—Boston selectmen issue call for Town Meeting next day to consider tea crisis.

November 5 (morning)—More than a thousand persons attend Town Meeting in Faneuil Hall, select committees to call on tea consignees and demand their resignations. Governor meets with Council, urges action to punish rioters who attacked Clarke warehouse, but fails. Council largely unsympathetic.

November 5 (afternoon)—Committee headed by John Hancock calls on Clarkes and Faneuil to demand resignations. Second committee rides to

Milton to make similar demand of Hutchinson brothers. Town Meeting declares Clarke and Faneuil reply to be "wholly unsatisfactory and daringly affrontive."

November 6 (morning)—Town Meeting reconvenes to hear Hutchinson reply, votes answer "entirely unsatisfactory and daringly affrontive." Cries of "To arms! To arms!" heard.

November 12—Governor Hutchinson orders John Hancock, as colonel of the Governor's Company of Cadets, to alert his militiamen to be ready to assemble, fully armed, on sudden call. Tension grows in Boston.

November 17—Jonathan Clarke arrives home from England. Street mob gathers outside Richard Clarke's residence that night and, after someone inside foolishly fires pistol, smashes all the windows and shutters.

November 19—Governor Hutchinson meets with Council, asks help in suppressing "all riotous assemblies of the people." Council is uncooperative. Hears petition from tea consignees, dated November 18th, asking that Governor and Council accept custody of tea cargoes when they arrive. Council refuses.

November 23—Richard Clarke leaves town for refuge somewhere in the countryside.

November 27 (morning)—Governor and Council fail to reach agreement on positive course of action to quell disturbances, punish rioters.

November 27 (evening)—Jonathan and Isaac Clarke, at their own request, meet privately with Boston's Board of Selectmen to try to resolve the crisis. Meeting breaks up with nothing resolved.

November 28—*Dartmouth*, first tea ship to arrive, anchors off Castle William, headquarters of British regiment stationed in Boston. Whole town aroused. Handbills call the citizenry to an emergency meeting next day in Faneuil Hall.

November 29 (morning)—Crowd far too large for Fanueil Hall gathers at 9 a.m., moves to Old South Church, a much roomier place of assembly. Hutchinson and Council meet at the same time. Mass meeting resolves that arriving tea must not be landed or pay duty, but be returned to England in vessels that brought it to Boston. Consignees given until 3 p.m. to agree.

November 29 (afternoon)—Tea consignees take refuge in Castle William, refuse demands of mass meeting. John Singleton Copley, son-in-law of Richard Clarke, volunteers to go to Castle and try to persuade consignees to change minds. Meeting votes to have volunteers guard tea ships around the clock, beginning that night.

November 30 (morning)—Copley brings slightly conciliatory message from consignees to reconvened mass meeting. Voters declare it unsatisfactory. Copley returns to Castle to try to persuade consignees to come before the meeting and state their case.

November 30 (afternoon)—Copley returns late, with consignees' refusal to appear. Their last message offers to place tea in storage, with town given right to inspect it at will. Meeting rejects offer. Captain Hall brings *Dartmouth* up to Rowe's Wharf.

December 1—*Dartmouth* ordered to warp around to Griffin's Wharf, with subsequent arrivals to follow suit, thus enabling one guard to watch all tea ships.

December 2—Tea ship *Eleanor* arrives and docks at Griffin's Wharf.

December 8—Brig *Beaver*, with tea cargo, arrives but goes at once into quarantine because of smallpox outbreak aboard. Governor Hutchinson asks Admiral Montagu to block harbor exits with warships so that no tea ship can escape without proper clearance.

December 10—Brig *William* runs aground on Cape Cod in gale; cargo salvageable.

December 14—Largest mass meeting ever assembled in Boston up to that time, comprising delegates from five towns, meets in Old South Church. Francis Rotch, owner of *Dartmouth,* told to apply to customhouse for clearance, at first refuses, and is then obliged to consent.

December 15—Rotch and escort, including Samuel Adams, return to customhouse, where Rotch is officially refused clearance for *Dartmouth* until duty is paid.

December 16 (morning)—Mass meeting reconvenes. After hearing report of Rotch's failed mission, orders him to go to Governor Hutchinson at Milton and demand pass for his ship to leave harbor.

December 16 (afternoon)—Rotch confers with Governor, who firmly rejects his appeal for a pass. Rotch reports to meeting. Samuel Adams declares, "This meeting can do nothing more to save the country." War whoops are heard at the church doors. Meeting adjourns abruptly.

December 16 (evening)—Boston Tea Party held, from 6 to 9 p.m.

December 23—Captain James Scott's *Hayley* departs for London, with Dr. Hugh Williamson, an eyewitness to the Tea Party, as passenger.

1774

January 9—Francis Rotch sails for England aboard *Dartmouth.*

January 19—Lord Dartmouth and King George III receive first news of Boston Tea Party; public reads about it three days later in London newspapers. Public and Parliament thoroughly angered. Latter determines to punish Boston.

Late January—Jonathan Clarke sails for London aboard Captain Coffin's *Beaver.*

February 19—Americans lately arrived in London from Boston are summoned to tell Privy Council all they know about the Tea Party. Their testimony spoils incipient government plans to try ringleaders on charges of high treason.

March 14—Lord North reads to House of Commons text of proposed Boston Port Bill, first of several Coercive Acts and designed to close Boston to ocean traffic until East India Company has been compensated for the destroyed tea. Transfers customhouse to Salem.

March 30—Boston Port Bill passed overwhelmingly by Parliament.

April 18—General Gage sails for Boston with troop replacements and rein-forcements to resume post as commander-in-chief of British troops in North America and to replace Governor Hutchinson while latter takes promised six months' leave in England.

May 10—Boston first reads full text of Boston Port Bill in newspapers; re-acts with dismay and anger.

May 11—Parliament passes coercive Regulating Bill, which alters Massachu-setts charter to take government out of the hands of its freeholders.

May 13—Town Meeting at Boston votes overwhelmingly to refuse to pay for the destroyed tea.

May 17—Governor Gage given correct but resentful reception in Boston.

May 18—Parliament passes coercive Justice Bill, which enables King to ap-point all judges, law officers, and juries, and, in effect, places province under martial law.

June 1—Boston Port Bill goes into effect. Governor Hutchinson departs for London.

Purported Participants in the
Boston Tea Party

In 1835, Benjamin B. Thatcher compiled a list of fifty-eight names of men who had almost certainly taken part in the Boston Tea Party. Seven of those men were still alive at that time, and helped him draw up his list. In 1884, Francis S. Drake added fifty names to Thatcher's list, basing his additions on family documents and traditions. He also made a sturdy effort to find out the birth dates and occupations not only of his own group of fifty but of Thatcher's group as well. He only partially succeeded.

Here, for the first time, the two lists are combined and arranged in alphabetical order, with ages and occupations given wherever available. One hundred and ten individuals are named, though contemporary estimates of the number of participants ran as high as two hundred.

The only well-known persons believed to have been present and active at Griffin's Wharf on the night of December 16, 1773, were William Molineux, the ill-tempered Irish merchant who had led the delegation to Richard Clarke's warehouse on the afternoon of November 3rd; Dr. Thomas Young, John Adams's close friend and family physician; and Paul Revere. As far as we know, Molineux, at fifty-seven, was the oldest man there. Dr. Young was forty-one. Revere was thirty-eight.

Nathaniel Barber, 45, merchant
Samuel Barnard, 36, occupation unknown
Henry Bass, 34, merchant
Edward Bates, age and occupation unknown
Thomas Boulter, 38, housewright
David Bradlee, 31, occupation unknown*
Josiah Bradlee, 19, ditto*
Nathaniel Bradlee, 27, ditto*
Thomas Bradlee, 29, ditto*
James Brewer, age unknown, pump and block maker
Seth Ingersoll Brown, 23, house carpenter
Stephen Bruce, age unknown, merchant

Benjamin Burton, 24, occupation unknown
Nicholas Campbell, 41, sailor
George Carleton, age and occupation unknown
Thomas Chase, age unknown, distiller
Benjamin Clarke, 18, cooper's apprentice
John Cochran, 23, occupation unknown
Gilbert Colesworthy, 28, occupation unknown
Gersham Collier, age and occupation unknown
Adam Collson, 35, leather dresser
James Foster Condy, age unknown, bookseller

S. Coolidge, age and occupation unknown

Samuel Cooper, 18, cooper's apprentice

John Crane, 29, house carpenter

Thomas Dana, Jr., age and occupation unknown

Robert Davis, 26, importer of groceries and liquors

Edward Dolbear, 18, cooper's apprentice

Joseph Eaton, age unknown, "an eccentric but amiable" hatter

Joseph Eayres, age unknown, housewright

——— Eckley, age unknown, barber

Benjamin Edes, age unknown, printer

William Etheridge, age unknown, mason

Samuel Fenno, 28, housewright

Samuel Foster, age and occupation unknown

Nathaniel Frothingham, 27, coachmaker

John Fulton, 30, brother-in-law of the Bradlees

John Gammell, 24, carpenter

Samuel Gore, 22, house painter, father was a Tory

Moses Grant, 30, upholsterer

John Greenleaf, age and occupation unknown

Samuel Hammond, 24, farmer

William Hendley, 25, mason

George R. T. Hewes, 31, shoemaker

John Hicks, 48, occupation unknown

Samuel Hobbs, 23, tanner's apprentice

John Hooton, 18, oarmaker's apprentice

Samuel Howard, 21, shipwright

Edward C. Howe, 31, ropemaker

Jonathan Hunnewell, 14

Richard Hunnewell, Jonathan's father, age unknown, mason

Richard Hunnewell, Jr., Jonathan's brother, 16, occupation unknown

Thomas Hunstable, 20, occupation unknown

Abraham Hunt, 25, wine merchant

David Ingersoll, 23, housewright

David Kennison, 37, farmer, lived to be 115

Joseph Lee, 28, merchant

Amos Lincoln, 20, housewright's apprentice

Matthew Loring, 23, leather worker

Joseph Lovering, 15, apprentice

Thomas Machin, 29, immigrant laborer from England

Ebenezer Mackintosh, 36, shoemaker

Archibald MacNeil, 23, occupation unknown

John May, 25, occupation unknown

——— Mead, age and occupation unknown

Thomas Melvill, 22, merchant's clerk

William Molineux, 57, merchant

Thomas Moore, 20, operator of a commercial wharf

Anthony Morse, age and occupation unknown

Joseph Mountford, 23, cooper

Eliphalet Newell, age and occupation unknown

Joseph Pearse Palmer, age unknown, importer and hardware merchant

Jonathan Parker, age unknown, farmer

Joseph Payson, 30, housewright

Samuel Peck, age unknown, cooper

John Peters, 41, occupation unknown

William Pierce, 29, barber

Lendall Pitts, 26, clerk of the market, officer in Hancock's Cadets

Samuel Pitts, age and occupation unknown

Thomas Porter, age unknown, merchant

Henry Prentiss, 24, occupation unknown

John Prince, 20, occupation unknown

Edward Proctor, 40, importer

Henry Purkitt, 18, cooper's apprentice

John Randall, 23, occupation unknown

Paul Revere, 38, silversmith and engraver

Joseph Roby, age and occupation unknown

John Russell, age unknown, mason

William Russell, 25, schoolteacher

Robert Sessions, 21, laborer

Joseph Shed, 41, carpenter

Benjamin Simpson, 17, bricklayer's apprentice

Peter Slater, 14, ropemaker's apprentice

Samuel Sprague, 19, mason's apprentice

John Spurr, 25, occupation unknown

James Starr, 32, French and Indian War veteran, occupation unknown

Phineas Stearns, 37, farmer and blacksmith

Ebenezer Stevens, 22, carpenter

Elisha Story, 30, physician

James Swan, 19, counting-house clerk

John Truman, age and occupation unknown

Thomas Urann, age unknown, ship joiner

Josiah Wheeler, 30, housewright

David Williams, age and occupation unknown

Isaac Williams, age and occupation unknown

Jeremiah Williams, age unknown, blacksmith

Thomas Williams, 19, apprentice

Nathaniel Willis, 18, printer's apprentice

Joshua Wyeth, 15, apprentice

Thomas Young, 41, physician

---

* David, Josiah, Nathaniel and Thomas Bradlee were brothers.

Guard Rosters for Tea Ship Dartmouth
(November 29-30, 1773)

NOVEMBER 29

Captain: Edward Proctor*

Benjamin Alley
Henry Bass*
Stephen Bruce*
Thomas Chase*
James Foster Condy*
John Crane*
Benjamin Edes*
Joseph Edwards
Moses Grant*
John Greenleaf*
James Henderson
Robert Hitchborn

Thomas Knox, Jr.
John Lovell
Joseph Lovering*
John McFadden
Joshua Pico
Joseph Pierce, Jr.
Paul Revere*
Captain Riordan
Jonathan Stodder
Dr. Elisha Story*
Josiah Wheeler*
John Winthrop

NOVEMBER 30

Captain: Ezekiel Cheever

Ebenezer Ayres
Rufus Bant
Thomas Bolley
James Brewer*
William Clap
Adam Collson*
Obadiah Curtis
William Dickman
Joseph Eayres*
William Elberson
Joseph Froude

Daniel Hewes
Richard Hunnewell*
Benjamin Ingerson
Samuel Peck*
Nicholas Pierce
George Ray
John Rice
Benjamin Stevens
William Sutton
Thomas Tileston
Thomas Urann*

* Took part in the Boston Tea Party.

Selective Notes on Sources

Throughout my text I have heavily mined Francis Drake's *Tea Leaves* for the contents of many letters written by or sent to various tea consignees, as well as for fragments of conversation reported in those letters that I could appropriate and transpose from third-person to first-person form. Drake also provided the texts of handbills and the contents of a good many letters sent to or by the East India Company officials. In the Prefatory Note to his book, published by subscription in 1884, he explained the interesting provenance of this prime material, which he, too, mined for his particular purposes.

"The collection of letters and documents which has occasioned the preparation of the present volume," Drake wrote, "was for many years, and until his decease, in the possession of Mr. Abel Bowen, a well-known engraver and publisher of Boston sixty years ago [1824], and was obtained by him from a person who procured it in Halifax, N.S., whither many valuable papers, both public and private, relating to New England were carried when in March, 1776, the British and Tories evacuated Boston." Bowen's daughters made the collection available to Drake, and historians have treated it as genuine. There seems to be no reasonable doubt of its authenticity, though I would like to know how the London items got to Halifax.

In the following paragraphs, I shall specifically cite only those important sources other than Drake. The reader sufficiently interested to rummage around in my sources will be able to find a good deal of my raw material in *Tea Leaves*. I have not attempted to point out the origins of quotations and factual material the source of which is self-evident, and to which the Bibliography is a more specific guide.

THE ANTAGONISTS

(1763—November 2, 1773)

The location and architectural particulars of Richard Clarke's residence came from a detailed footnote on page 85 of Volume 8, *Transactions* of the Colonial Society of Massachusetts, 1902–04, hereinafter referred to as CSM *Transactions*.

The interesting fact that John Robinson, Secretary to the Treasury, sent advance instructions to Boston's customs men to accommodate the tea consignees in every way possible was found on page 25 of Bernard Donoughue's invaluable *British Politics and the American Revolution*.

Details of typical transatlantic trading vessels of those days, and specific tonnages, derive from young Samuel Eliot Morison's 1922 paper on "The Commerce of Boston on the Eve of the Revolution" for the American Antiquarian Society.

The prediction in a London newspaper, brought to Boston on the *Hayley* by Captain Scott, that "accidents" would destroy the tea ships was reprinted in the Boston *Gazette* on Monday, November 22, 1773.

Details of the doings of Ebenezer Mackintosh, the Loyal Nine, and especially of "O.C., *Sec'y*," came from papers by George P. Anderson, printed in Volume 26, *Transactions* of the Colonial Society of Massachusetts, 1924–26.

The concluding quotation from Governor Thomas Hutchinson about Samuel Adams was picked up from John C. Miller's *Sam Adams: Pioneer in Propaganda,* and came originally from the Massachusetts Archives.

BRICKBATS AND PAPER SKIRMISHES

(November 3, 1773—December 16, 1773)

The text of Governor Hutchinson's letter of November 15th to Lord Dartmouth was found on pages 164–66, Volume 13, *Proceedings* of the Massachusetts Historical Society, 1873–75, hereinafter identified as MHS *Proceedings.*

The Boston *Gazette*'s description of the mob attack on Richard Clarke's residence on the night of November 17th was not printed until Monday, December 13th—a mysterious delay. The Clarkes' own terse, unpunctuated version of the same affair was taken from page 84, CSM *Transactions.* The tea consignees' formal, negative reply of November 18th to the Town Meeting's demand for more specific information about the tea shipments came from the same source. So did Richard Clarke's letter of November 23rd to his sons bowing out of the tea dispute, which was printed on pages 87–88 of that source.

John Scollay's description of the November 27th conference of Jonathan and Isaac Clarke with the full Board of Selectmen of Boston was contained in his very important letter of December 23rd to Arthur Lee. That letter covered all the principal events leading up to the Tea Party, and the Party itself. It was printed in full on pages 379–86 of Volume 4, Series IV, of the *Collections* of the Massachusetts Historical Society, 1858.

The journal of the *Dartmouth* was printed in an appendix to Benjamin Thatcher's otherwise highly dubious *Traits of the Tea Party,* a nonogenarian's hazy but boastful recollections, printed in 1835.

The fact that Dr. Joseph Warren and Dr. Benjamin Church drafted the urgent appeal of November 29th to the neighboring Committees of Correspondence to join Boston in a mass meeting that day, and the fact that Warren wrote the first half and Church the last, were gleaned from page 255 of Frothingham's *Life and Times of Joseph Warren* (1865) and from pages 167–8 of MHS *Proceedings*.

Governor Hutchinson's written commentary on the character of the mass meetings of November 29th and 30th was excerpted from a December 2nd letter of his to Lord Dartmouth, quoted on page 300 of Hosmer's *Life of Thomas Hutchinson*. His letter to Governor Tryon, including the quotation "Nothing can be more inflammatory . . . ," was written on December 1st and also quoted in Hosmer's *Life,* page 299. In this same letter Hutchinson announced that he had sent an order to Colonel Leslie, at the Castle, to shelter the tea consignees.

John Singleton Copley's long, frequently misspelled letter to the Clarke brothers at the Castle, describing his report to the mass meeting and warning them to avoid having anything to do with the Governor, was written December 1st and printed on pages 211–13 of the *Copley-Pelham Letters,* published by the Massachusetts Historical Society in 1914.

The Boston Selectmen's stern instructions to the keeper of the quarantine hospital on Rainsford Island, where the *Beaver* put in on arrival, were printed in a footnote on page 267 of Frothingham's book on Warren.

The text of Thomas Hutchinson, Jr.'s letter of December 14th to his youngest brother (not to Elisha, as the source said, for Elisha then was still with him at the Castle) came from page 96 of the *Diary and Letters of Thomas Hutchinson,* edited by the latter's grandson.

Governor Hutchinson described Francis Rotch's lonely mission to Milton on the afternoon of December 16th both in his *History* (page 435) and in a contemporary letter to Israel Mauduit, reproduced on pages 170–1 of MHS *Proceedings*.

Details of the sunset hour and tide state, as well as the phase of the moon, for December 16th came from Ames's 1773 *Almanack*.

All that survives of Josiah Quincy, Jr.'s impressive speech to the crowd in Old South Church late that afternoon comes from pages LIX and LX of the Introduction to *Tea Leaves*.

MINGLING TEA WITH SEA WATER

(December 16, 1773: 6–9 P.M.)

The description of the Boston Tea Party is based almost wholly on the various firsthand accounts gathered by Drake for *Tea Leaves*. Additional sources are self-explanatory, except for that colorful bit of verse beginning "What discontents, what dire events . . . ," which appeared originally in the *New-Hampshire Gazette* of September 12, 1776. I found it in a footnote on page 282 of Frothingham's book on Warren.

Dr. Williamson's testimony about the Tea Party before the King's Privy Council was printed on pages 386–89 of the 1858 volume of *Collections* of the Massachusetts Historical Society.

PAYING THE FIDDLER

(December 17, 1773—June 1, 1774)

Hutchinson's statement that he dispatched expresses before sunrise on the day following the Tea Party, and his subsequent short description of what happened the night before, were printed on pages 172–3 of MHS *Proceedings.* Samuel Adams's summary of the Tea Party came from page 72, Volume III, of Harry Alonzo Cushing's edition of *The Writings of Samuel Adams,* 1907.

The excerpt from Hutchinson's letter to Mauduit, commenting sarcastically that "Adams [Sam] never was in greater glory," was quoted on page 304 of Hosmer's *Life of Thomas Hutchinson.*

The long John Adams quote from his letter of December 17th to James Warren came from pages 333–4 of the Charles Francis Adams edition (1854) of the *Life and Works of John Adams.* The letter of December 22nd is taken from page 335 of the same source.

Governor Hutchinson's letter of December 23rd to Isaac Williams came from pages 303–04 of Hosmer's *Life.* Samuel Adams's letter to Arthur Lee describing the "height of joy" in Boston was printed on pages 73–77 of the Cushing edition of Adams's *Writings,* where it was incorrectly dated December 31st, probably owing to a typographical error, since internal evidence makes it clear that the letter went off on Hancock's *Hayley* on the 23rd. Joseph Warren's letter to Arthur Lee, dispatched the same day on the same ship, came from pages 288–9 of Frothingham's *Life.*

The Hutchinson letter to the Scottish historian William Robertson was quoted on page 304 of the Hosmer *Life,* and his letter to Samuel Swift on pages 304–05 of the same source.

Captain Scott's subdued but dramatically evocative account of the wretched eastward voyage of the *Hayley* in January, 1774, was quoted originally on page 277 of Baxter's *The House of Hancock.*

Benjamin Franklin's gentle appraisal of Lord Dartmouth came from a letter to his son, written July 14, 1773, and printed on page 154 of Bigelow's edition of Franklin's *Works.*

The silly rumor about the fish in Boston Harbor tasting of tea came from a late January, 1774, entry in *An Eighteenth Century Journal (1774–76),* compiled by John Hampden.

Sam Adams's scornful remark about Franklin's clumsiness as a politician was quoted on page 265 of Hosmer's book on Adams.

Tom Hutchinson's letter of January 9, 1774, to his brother Elisha, by then free of the Castle, was printed in *Diary and Letters of Thomas Hutchinson,* page 97. So, too, on successive pages, were his letters of January 21st and February 4th.

John Adams's bored description of Boston's mood on April 9th—"Still! silent as midnight!," etc.—was printed on page 295 of Frothingham's book on Warren, but came originally from page 324, Volume 2, *Life and Works of John Adams.*

Details of the Parliamentary maneuvers and reactions following news of the Boston Tea Party derive mostly from Donoughue's *British Politics and the American Revolution,* but Colonel Isaac Barré's eloquent speech of April 15th was found in its entirety in the April, 1774, issue of *The Gentleman's Magazine,* pages 166-9.

Final quotes from Sam Adams pertaining to the passage of the Boston Port Bill, and coverage of the arrival of General Gage and the departure of Governor Hutchinson, were found in Hosmer's *Samuel Adams,* pages 270-83.

APPENDIXES

The *Dartmouth* guard rosters for November 29-30, 1773, came from *Tea Leaves.* I added information to the age groups of Purported Participants in the Boston Tea Party from scattered biographical evidence contained in the same source.

Bibliography

Adams, John, Life and Works of, with a Life of the Author by his grandson, Charles Francis Adams, vol. IX. Little, Brown & Co., Boston, 1854.

Ames, Nathaniel, An Astronomical Diary; or, An Almanack for the Year of Our Lord, 1773. Boston, 1773.

Anderson, George P., "Ebenezer Mackintosh: Stamp Act Rioter and Patriot," pp. 15–64, March, 1924; "A Note on Ebenezer Mackintosh," pp. 348–361, Feb. 1926; Transactions, 1924–26, v. 26. Publications of the Colonial Society of Massachusetts, Boston, 1927.

Andrews, John, Letters of (1772–76), pp. 316–412, vol. 1864–65, Proceedings of the Massachusetts Historical Society, 1865.

Bargar, B.D., Lord Dartmouth and the American Revolution. The University of South Carolina Press, Columbia, S.C., 1965.

Baxter, William T., The House of Hancock. Harvard University Press, Cambridge, 1945.

Bigelow, John, ed., The Complete Works of Benjamin Franklin, vol. V. G.P. Putnam's Sons, New York, 1887.

Boston Gazette and Country Journal, The, August 16–December 27, 1773, printed by Edes & Gill, in Queen-Street, Boston, 1773.

Bowen, Catherine Drinker, John Adams and the American Revolution. Little, Brown & Co., Boston, 1950.

"Boyle's Journal of Occurrences in Boston," vol. 84, New England Historical and Genealogical Register, Boston, 1930.

Bridenbaugh, Carl, Cities in Revolt; Urban Life in America, 1743–76. Alfred A. Knopf, New York, 1955.

Butterfield, L.H., ed., The Adams Papers, v. 1, Adams Family Correspondence, 1761–76; v. 2, Diary and Autobiography of John Adams, 1771–81. The Belknap Press of Harvard University Press, Cambridge, 1963.

Butterworth, Hezekiah, Young Folks History of Boston. Estes and Lauriat, Boston, 1881.

Copley-Pelham Letters, vol. 71. Collections of the Massachusetts Historical Society, 1914.

Crawford, Mary Caroline, Old Boston Days and Ways. Little, Brown & Co., Boston, 1909.

Curwen, Samuel, Journal and Letters of the Late, with Biographical Notices of Many American Loyalists and Other Eminent Persons, by George Atkinson Ward, of the New-York Historical Society. C.S. Francis & Co., New York, 1842.

Cushing, Harry Alonzo, ed., The Writings of Samuel Adams, v. III. G.P. Putnam's Sons, New York, 1907.

Davidson, Philip, *Propaganda and the American Revolution, 1763–83.* University of N. Carolina Press, Chapel Hill, 1941.

Deacon Tudor's Diary; or, Memorandums from 1709, etc., by John Tudor, to 1775 & 1778, 1780 and to '93; edited by William Tudor, A.B. Press of Wallace Spooner, Boston, 1896.

"Destruction of the Tea in the Harbor of Boston, Dec. 16, 1773," *Collections of the Massachusetts Historical Society,* 4th series, v. IV (1858).

Dictionary of American Biography, v. 5. Charles Scribner's Sons, New York.

Dictionary of National Biography, v. 13. Oxford University Press.

Donoughue, Bernard, *British Politics and the American Revolution. The Path to War, 1773–75.* Macmillan & Co., Ltd., London, 1964.

Drake, Francis S., *Tea Leaves.* A.O. Crane, Boston, 1884.

Drake, Samuel Adams, *Old Landmarks and Historic Personages of Boston.* Little, Brown & Co., Boston, 1900.

Flexner, James Thomas, *John Singleton Copley.* Houghton Mifflin Co., The Riverside Press, Cambridge, 1948.

Forbes, Esther, *Paul Revere and the World He Lived In.* Houghton Mifflin Co., Boston, 1942.

Frothingham, Richard, *Life and Times of Joseph Warren.* Little, Brown & Co., Boston, 1865.

Gentleman's Magazine, The; February, March, and April, 1774. London.

Guedalla, Philip, *Fathers of the Revolution.* G.P. Putnam's Sons, New York & London, 1926.

Hampden, John, compiler, *An Eighteenth Century Journal (1774–76).* Macmillan & Co., Ltd., London, 1940.

Hosmer, James K., *The Life of Thomas Hutchinson.* Houghton, Mifflin & Co., The Riverside Press, Cambridge, 1896.

———, *Samuel Adams.* Houghton, Mifflin & Co., Boston, 1886.

Hulton, Ann, *Letters of a Loyalist Lady;* Being the Letters of Ann Hulton, sister of Henry Hulton, Commissioner of Customs at Boston, 1767–1776. Harvard University Press, Cambridge, 1927.

Hutchinson, Thomas, *The Diary and Letters of His Excellency Thomas Hutchinson, Esq.,* compiled by Peter Orlando Hutchinson, one of his great-grandsons. Sampson Low, Marston, Searle & Rivington, London, 1883.

———, *History of the Province of Massachusetts Bay, 1749–74;* comprising a Detailed Narrative of the Origin and Early Stages of the American Revolution. John Murray, London, 1828.

Knollenberg, Bernhard, "Did Samuel Adams Provoke the Boston Tea Party and the Clash at Lexington?" *Proceedings of the American Antiquarian Society,* v. 70 (1960), Worcester, Mass., 1961.

Labaree, Benjamin Woods, *The Boston Tea Party.* Oxford University Press, 1964.

Lossing, Benson J., *The Pictorial Field-Book of the Revolution,* v. 1. Harper & Brothers, N.Y., 1855.

Miller, John C., *Sam Adams, Pioneer in Propaganda*. Little, Brown & Co., Boston, 1936.

Morison, Samuel Eliot, "The Commerce of Boston on the Eve of the Revolution," v. 32. *Proceedings of the American Antiquarian Society*, April–October, 1922.

————, *The Oxford History of the American People*. Oxford University Press, 1965.

North, Lord, "Lord North, the Prime Minister: A Personal Memoir," Part II; *The Gentleman's Magazine*, August, 1903, pp. 260–277.

Pierce, Edward L., "Recollections as a Source of History," *Proceedings of the Massachusetts Historical Society*, v. 10, Second Series (1895–6), pp. 473–490.

Publications of the Colonial Society of Massachusetts, v. 8; Transactions, 1902–04; documents from the Richard Clarke papers, Boston, 1906.

Ross, Marjorie Drake, *The Book of Boston: The Colonial Period*. Hastings House, 1960.

Rowe, John, *Letters and Diary of John Rowe, Boston Merchant*, ed. by Anne Rowe Cunningham. W.B. Clarke Co., Boston, 1903.

Ryerson, Egerton, *The Loyalists of America and Their Times, 1620–1816*. William Briggs, Toronto, 1880.

Schlesinger, Arthur M., *The Colonial Merchants and the American Revolution*. Facsimile Library, Inc., New York, 1939.

Smith, Page, *John Adams*, v. 1, 1735–1784. Doubleday & Co., Inc., Garden City, N.Y., 1962.

Stark, James H., *The Loyalists of Massachusetts and the Other Side of the American Revolution*. W.B. Clarke Co., Boston, 1907.

"Summary of American Advices on Tea-Ships," *The Gentleman's Magazine*, May, 1774, pp. 26–28.

"Tea-Party Anniversary," *Proceedings of the Massachusetts Historical Society*, v. 13 (1873–75), pp. 151–215.

Thatcher, Benjamin B., *Traits of the Tea Party;* Being a Memoir of George R. T. Hewes. Harper & Brothers, N.Y., 1835.

Trumbull, John, Autobiography, Reminiscences and Letters of, from 1756 to 1841. Wiley & Putnam, New York and London, 1841.

Walpole, Horace, *Journal of the Reign of King George the Third, from the Year 1771 to 1783*. Ed., with notes, by Dr. John Doran. R. Bentley, London, 1859.

————, *The Last Journals of,* During the Reign of George III, from 1771–1783, with Notes by Dr. Doran; edited with an introduction by A. Francis Steuart, v. 1. John Lane Company, London, 1910.

Warden, G.B., *Boston, 1689–1776*. Little, Brown & Co., Boston, 1970.

Warren-Adams Letters, v. 1, 1743–1777, Massachusetts Historical Society Collections, v. 72, 1917.

Warren, Mercy, *History of the Rise, Progress, and Termination of the American Revolution*, v. 1. Manning & Loring, Boston, 1805.

Whitehill, Walter Muir, *Boston, A Topographical History*. Belknap Press, Harvard; Cambridge, 1968.

Wickwire, Franklin B., *British Subministers and Colonial America*. Princeton University Press, 1966.

Illustration Credits

Index

Index

Welles, Henry, 19, 21
Wheeler, Josiah, 106, 143, 144
Wheler, Edward, 49, 50, 117
Whig(s), *see esp.* 14, 17, 19, 33, 34, 53,
    63, 67, 78, 81, 83, 109, 112, 124, 130,
    131, 132, 152
Williams, Isaac, 112, 143, 148
Williams, Jonathan, xiv, 67, 125

Williamson, Dr. Hugh, xiv, 100, 113, 115,
    125, 139, 147
William, the, 13, 86, 108, 137, 139
Winslow, Joshua, 10, 12, 16, 31, 44, 63,
    117, 137
Wyeth, Joshua, 100, 101, 104, 122, 143

Young, Dr. Thomas, xiv, 70, 92, 125, 141,
    143

Roxbury.